PAUL: PORTRAIT OF A REVOLUTIONARY

Other books by Donald Coggan

DONALD COGGAN

PAUL: PORTRAIT OF A REVOLUTIONARY

HODDER AND STOUGHTON
LONDON SYDNEY AUCKLAND TORONTO

British Library Cataloguing in Publication Data

Coggan, Donald
  Paul : portrait of a revolutionary.
  1. Paul, *the Apostle, Saint* 2. Christian
  saints——Turkey——Tarsus——Biography
  3. Tarsus (Turkey)——Biography
  I. Title
  225.9′24   BS2506

  ISBN 0–340–39822–1

In thankfulness to God
for many friends,
throughout the Anglican Communion
and beyond it,
who have enriched my ministry
over fifty years
1934–1984

CONTENTS

After a long silence, Borodin, still gazing out of the window, began murmuring, half to himself. "You know," he mused, "I used to read the New Testament. Again and again I read it. It is the most wonderful story ever told. That man Paul. He was a *real* revolutionary. I take off my hat to him!" He made a symbolic gesture, his long black hair falling momentarily over his long face.

Another long silence . . .

Quoted from John McCook Roots: *Chou: An informal Biography of China's Legendary Chou En-Lai* (Doubleday and Co Inc, New York, 1978). The author is reporting on a conversation between himself and Mikhail M. Borodin, Soviet Mission Chief under Lenin.

INTRODUCTION

A member of the Amadeus Quartet, during the course of a television interview with Bernard Levin, was speaking of the effect on him and his colleagues of constantly rehearsing and performing the works of Beethoven over the thirty-five years of their work together. He said: "I feel that he (Beethoven) is one of us." He spoke, too, of their *reverence* for Mozart acquired during those years of studying, performing and interpreting his works.

Taking these remarks in inverse order, it is doubtful whether the writings of Paul will yield their depths to the reader unless there be on his part an element of *reverence* as he studies them. After all, they have been a stable part of the Church's liturgical reading for the best part of two millennia. They have been the stay and nourishment of millions of Christians who have lived by their truths and died in their strength and, dying, have entered into life.

But can we say of Paul, as members of the Quartet said of Beethoven, that we "feel he is one of us"? In the case of many readers, the answer is 'yes'. The long interval of the centuries is transcended, and they find themselves in the company of one who was a disciple of Jesus as they themselves are, too. The study of Paul leads them into a deeper obedience to Christ, and that results in a growing sense of unity with the apostle.

But for others that is simply not true. It is for people such as these that this book is written. I have in mind clergy whose difficulty with Paul is reflected in the rarity of the occasions on which they preach from his writings and the timidity with which they expound them. If this is true of the clergy, is it not equally true of Readers? I have also in mind those lay men and women who would like to understand the apostle and his writings, what it was that 'made him tick', and what was at the heart of his mission and message, but who have been put off and have abandoned their search. The causes for this abandonment are many – dry-as-dust school lessons on the journeys of Paul, difficult passages read (often with little interest or comprehension) as lections in church, the immense differences in outlook between first-century writer and twentieth-century reader, and so on.

This book does not set out to be a commentary on the Pauline epistles. Of such commentaries there is an abundance, written for every variety of reader. Rather, it attempts to be an introduction to the *man*, a portrait of a revolutionary, a man in Christ, a pilgrim-apostle, a man on the road – not only the road which led from Jerusalem to Rome, but also the road which led from earth to heaven. Paul's was a pilgrim's progress. If the reading of this book were to enable some to fall into step with the apostle on the journey, so that in some sense he became "one of us", the writer would be well content.

The writing of this book has been an attempt in some small way to repay the author's debt to a man whose life and letters have been a constant challenge to him and a never-ending source of inspiration for preaching and lecturing. A recent journey following the tracks of the apostle through Ephesus, Iconium, Tarsus, Miletus, Corinth, Athens and Rome, has only served to deepen a sense of admiration and respect for this intrepid follower of Jesus.

The reading of this book will, of course, involve us in the careful study of many passages in the epistles, but I have sought generally to avoid the discussion of details of scholarship. I have relegated to the end of the book most of the references, in the hope that this method will enable the reader who wants to progress without interruption to do so, and the reader who wants to pursue deeper study to find helpful sources. The fairly frequent references to post-biblical and modern writers may help us to see in this first-century disciple of Jesus one who is truly "one of us" and one with us in struggle, in sorrow, in joy and in hope. After all, if Beethoven became a fifth to the Amadeus Quartet, why should not Paul become "one of us" by the power of the Spirit moving mind and will?

Most of the biblical quotations are from the New English Bible, though often I have noted other translations when they serve to clarify the points which I am concerned to make.

A considerable part of chapter 11 has already appeared in print as the Olivier Béguin Memorial Lecture, 1982, which I was privileged to deliver on behalf of the Bible Society of Australia, in the cities of Sydney, Canberra, Launceston and Melbourne. I am grateful to the Rev James R. Payne for permission to use it here.

My deepest thanks go to my wife Jean, who has shared my ministry for nearly fifty years, and has patiently watched the growth of this book.

I am very grateful to Mrs Rebecca Barker who has spent many hours in deciphering my manuscript and, through her typing, has brought order out of chaos. Any errors that remain are mine, not hers.

The Conversion of St Paul,   DONALD COGGAN
25 January, 1984   Sissinghurst
                              Kent

ACKNOWLEDGEMENTS

Extract from *The Conversion of SP* (Sir John Betjeman: Collected Poems) reproduced by permission of John Murray publishers Ltd.

Quotation from *A Sleep of Prisoners* (Christopher Fry, 1951) reproduced by permission of Oxford University Press.

Extract from "The Wild Knight" by G K Chesterton taken from The Collected Poems of G K Chesteron reproduced by permission of Miss D E Collins.

Extract from "Dunamis" by G Betty Hares reproduced with her permission.

Extract from "To Bring the Dead to Life" by Robert Graves taken from Collected Poems 1975 reproduced by permission of Robert Graves.

Front Cover photograph by permission © Scala/ Firenze.

                    the communication
Of the dead is tongued with fire beyond the language of
                        the living.

                                                    T. S. Eliot

                To bring the dead to life
                Is no great magic.
                Few are wholly dead:
                Blow on a dead man's embers
                And a live flame will start.

                                            Robert Graves

A book begins with falling in love. You lose your heart
to a place, a house, an avenue of trees, or with a
character who walks in and takes sudden and complete
possession of you. Imagination glows, and there is the
seed of your book.

                Elizabeth Goudge: *The Joy of the Snow*.
                                    An Autobiography

Now I seized greedily upon the adorable writing of your
Spirit, and especially upon the Apostle Paul . . . in that
pure eloquence I saw one Face, and I learned to rejoice
with trembling.

                        The Confessions of St Augustine

I knocked importunately at Paul in this place (i.e. Rom.
1: 17), thirsting most ardently to know what St Paul
meant.

                                    Martin Luther: *Works*

ABBREVIATIONS

AV	Authorised (King James Version) of the English Bible (1611)
Moffatt	A New Translation of the Bible, translated by James Moffatt (1926)
NEB	New English Bible (1961 and 1970)
Phillips	New Testament in Modern English, translated by J. B. Phillips (1958)
RSV	Revised Standard Version (1946–1952)
RV	Revised Version (1881–1885)

YOUTH

I am a Jew, a Tarsian from Cilicia, a citizen of no mean city.

Acts 21: 39

Israelite by race . . . a Hebrew born and bred.

Philippians 3: 5

I was born a [Roman] citizen.

Acts 22: 28

There was a time when, in the absence of law, I was fully alive; but when the commandment came, sin sprang to life and I died.

Romans 7: 9

1

YOUTH

Young Saul of Tarsus stood at the point where two rivers met. The first was the river of Judaism – narrow, deep, powerful. The second was the river of the outer world, the broad, open stream of Greek culture (all that is included in the word "Hellenism") and Roman power. The two rivers met in the important city of Tarsus where Saul was born. He found himself, through no choice of his own, to be the heir of two great traditions. He was a citizen of two worlds. His inheritance was exciting, even heady. It would have been easy to lose his footing and to be drowned at the confluence of the rivers. That he survived and indeed made something positive out of the very dangers of his position says much for the character of the man concerned.

Some understanding of these two cultures, the Graeco-Roman and the Jewish, is essential if we are to appreciate the man who stood at their confluence. To change the metaphor in terms of the title of this book, a portrait must be set against its proper background.

Let us look first, then, at the broad stream of the Graeco-Roman world of the first century AD.

On the outside cover of John Buchan's *Augustus*[1] are the words *immensa Romanae pacis majestas*. They also appear on the title-page. The phrase owes its origin to the elder Pliny,[2] and is worth quoting if only for the lovely rhythm of its syllables. But its value lies deeper than its linguistic beauty. "The unthinkable majesty of the Roman peace" was a reality of vast benefit to the people of the Empire. Having given the world a formal peace, Augustus was largely responsible for the re-building of that world, establishing the state firm and

17

secure and enthroning peace, security, law and a decent freedom.

Milton was to catch the feel of the *pax Romana* when he wrote:

No war or battle sound
Was heard the world around:
The idle spear and shield were high uphung;
The hookèd chariot stood
Unstained with hostile blood;
The trumpet spake not to the armèd throng;
And kings sat still with awful eye
As if they surely knew their sovran Lord was by.[3]

Adopting the title "princeps" as the one he most favoured, the aim of Augustus was to be First Citizen and principal servant – the man who, as John Buchan puts it, was a "modest, constitutionally minded citizen – the master of Egypt and its wealth, a god incarnate to three-fourths of mankind, the commander of 300,000 veterans, the undisputed ruler of the world".[4]

Something of the magnitude of the Empire over which Augustus presided can be seen if we bear in our mind's eye a land-mass whose frontiers were to the west the Atlantic, to the south the African desert, and to the north and east the Danube, the Rhine and the Euphrates. In the midst lay the huge "lake" of the Mediterranean Sea.

Something of the power of the man at the centre of this Empire can be seen when we note that "the First Citizen or *princeps* . . . was a superman . . . It had long been customary to build temples and offer sacrifices to rulers in the Near East; now such honours were paid to the Emperor – oaths were taken by his *genius*, the divinity in him or with him, and sacrifices and prayers and ceremonies and dedications of buildings beyond number were made in his honour."[5] It was during Augustus' life-time (63 BC–AD 14) that Paul was born. His debt to Augustus and his *pax Romana* was incalculable, for it meant that, as a boy, he could profit from intercourse with all kinds of men and minds, and as a man he could travel the world without let or hindrance created by war.

Augustus was himself a debtor to Alexander the Great, whose conquering journeys had taken him through Greece, Egypt and the Persian Empire, before he died in the year 323 BC at the age of thirty-three. It is true that his great Empire fell apart after his death, but he left behind him a unifying force the influence of which was to last for centuries – it was the Greek language. As Augustus surveyed the peoples of the Mediterranean basin, the vast majority of them, if they could not speak Greek with any measure of fluency, could understand it, and understanding it, found a measure of unity with their neighbours.

> The Babel of tongues was hushed
> In the beautiful language of Greece.

Even in that turbulent corner of the Empire where Jews tenaciously hung on to their sacred Hebrew language, the language of prophets and of liturgy, Greek was understood by many if not most – only across the narrow divide of the Jordan was the Decapolis, the "decade" of towns whose very name, the Decapolis, means just that. Greek was the *lingua franca*, in much the same way that English was the common language at the zenith of the British Empire – a bond of understanding, an answer to Babel.

Nock sums it up well: "All over the Near East the language of cultivated men was Greek. Roman officials and Roman colonies used also Latin for formal purposes, but did not confine themselves to it even for them. Native languages belonged to the uncultivated folk and above all to country dwellers."[6]

If young Saul of Tarsus, growing up as Augustus was growing old, owed him a debt for the *pax Romana*, he began to realise, Hebrew though he was, that he owed an equal if not greater debt to Alexander the Great. For Rome was the heir of Greek culture and thought, and Saul must have had many young friends who shared with him some of those insights, some of that beauty, as he shared with them the religious depths of his Hebrew faith. Later on, he must often have thanked God that, on his missionary journeys, he could make himself almost universally understood, not by using the language of his youthful upbringing, but by speaking (and writing) the gracious and delicate language of Greek.

A network of roads such as the world had never previously known – this was another of Rome's great gifts to civilisation. The policing of these roads by the Roman legions lent a measure of safety in travel which was a new factor, and one of incalculable benefit to a man on an errand such as Paul's. "A *measure* of safety" – the term is a comparative one. Not even Rome could ensure the banning of brigands from the highways and byways, and Paul was to suffer at their rough hands – what fierce encounters, one wonders, lay behind the brief "dangers from robbers" which he includes in the list of his sufferings in 2 Corinthians 11: 26? But John Buchan can claim that, as a result of the achievements of Augustus, "on land a journey was probably speedier and more certain in the civilised countries than at any time before the age of steam" (Paul did not travel only in "civilised" countries!), and "communications by sea were as fast as anything known in Europe before the nineteenth century".[7] It was no small feat to put down banditry and to drive the pirates from the seas.

Of these benefits, Saul must have become increasingly aware as adolescence gave place to manhood. He was glad of the contact they gave him with the minds of men of races other than his own. He was grateful for Rome's protection when he travelled to Jerusalem. Later, as a messenger of the Gospel, these benefits made possible journeys which took him from Jerusalem as far as Rome and conceivably (for history is uncertain at this point) to Spain. Certainly it was his ambition, his full intention, to go that far west – "I have been longing for many years to visit you on my way to *Spain*", he wrote to the Christians in Rome; "for I hope to see you *as I travel through*".[8]

If Shakespeare was right in making Brutus say:

> There is a tide in the affairs of men,
> Which, taken at the flood, leads on to fortune,[9]

Paul was even more to the point when he wrote of a tide in the affairs of *God* – "when the time had fully come, God sent forth his Son".[10] The world was exactly ready for the great Advent. God is never premature, never late. Multitudes of intelligent men and women, tired of the myths of ancient Greece and Rome, doubtful of the "mysteries" of the new religions and cults, were seeking for a deliverance which would save them from a sense of fatuity and hopelessness – how exactly Paul was to describe their world as "a world without hope and without God"![11] Not "without *gods*", for they abounded in almost every street of the big cities – there were "gods many and lords many", as he wrote to the Corinthians.[12] But "without *God*", yes. There was a longing, often imprecise and ill-defined but none the less real, for one God, and, further, for a monotheism which was deeply ethical and could command the respect of thoughtful minds and the assent of tender consciences. Wistfully, many such people looked towards the religion of the Jews, whose passionate monotheism and lofty ethics as taught by their prophets drew forth a stream of enquirers. These "God-fearers", as they were called, were able to learn much from what they heard in the synagogues, which sprang up in a kind of mushroom growth in the towns of the Graeco-Roman world, wherever there were ten adult male Jews of a mind to found such a nucleus. They listened to the Scriptures now translated into Greek (the so-called Septuagint, because tradition had it that seventy men had carried out the work of translation). They imbibed the teaching of the prophets. They listened, often with awe, to the warnings of judgement on those who followed false gods. Some of them went the whole way and became in everything but nationality Jews, followers of the one and all-holy Yahweh. Others could not face the strange rite of circumcision, nor take their share in the bloody round of animal sacrifice; but, apart from these matters, they gave their assent to a religion which was so markedly superior to those in which they had themselves been reared.

It was from people such as these that many of Paul's disciples were to come, for, though he preached a Messiah who had already arrived, been crucified and raised from the dead, the roots of his religion went down deep into Jewish soil.

The moment was indeed ripe for the Advent of Christ and for the proclamation of his message throughout the world.

Tarsus was no backwater. Far from it. Today it is a town of no great distinction, a commercial centre with few visible reminders of the man whose birth there, about the beginning of the Christian era, was to make it known throughout the world and down the centuries. Even its river Cydnus, which once bore on its waters Mark Antony and Cleopatra in all her glory in 41 BC, no longer flows through it. The little green, tranquil stream, which flows by Justinian's bridge on the outskirts of the town, is a kind of residual by-pass of the ancient river. But at the time of Saul's birth, Tarsus was "no mean city" – so he was to describe it, with pride, to the Roman tribune before whom he appeared.[13] The capital of the Roman province of Cilicia, its university compared very favourably with that of Athens, the main difference being that most of the students at Tarsus came from places nearby, whereas Athens drew them from afar. It was a distinguished centre of Greek culture, including Greek games, the gymnasium and the palaestra (or training place for athletes). Cilicia was a centre for the production of *cilicium*, the hair-cloth out

22

of which tents were made, a handcraft which Saul learnt and practised.[14] (Had not the Rabbis said that "he who does not teach his son a trade teaches him to be a thief"?) Traders bore their merchandise to it, and with the merchandise came the news of the world's happenings. Philosophers debated on its streets and Stoicism flourished there – if a man wanted to know the secret of self-improvement and the way to perfection, he would not lack Stoic teachers in Tarsus.

So "the broad, open river of Greek culture and Roman power" flowed majestically through Tarsus, and no youngster, least of all a highly intelligent one like Saul, could fail to be influenced by it. Which brings us to the other stream we mentioned – "the narrow, deep, and very powerful stream" of Judaism.

It cannot have been easy to be the parents of such a boy as Saul in such a place at such a time. They must have become aware very early that theirs was no ordinary son. Hugh Montefiore describes the mental make-up of the adult Paul in these words: "Paul had insight, and a leaping, darting mind. His intellect was pugnacious, and it functioned intuitively", and he goes on to speak of his method of teaching as one which "provides us with brilliant epigrams, memorable aphorisms, incisive battle thrusts".[15] One has only to read his letters to see the accuracy of Montefiore's description. As the parents watched their boy, thus equipped, ripen from childhood through adolescence to young manhood, they must have been proud and at the same time deeply anxious. Had they been living in Jerusalem, it would have been easier to ensure his continuance in the orthodoxy of their fathers and of their own faith, for every stone in Jerusalem spoke of their sacred history, and the Temple epitomised the worship of their jealous and loving God. In Tarsus, they had their synagogue, the centre of their weekly worship, the place where the Law was read and expounded, where justice was administered, and where the young men were brought up in the faith of their fathers. That meant much. But however

23

hard the parents tried, it was impossible to shield the growing lad from the winds of the pagan society which blew on him. Was there not a gymnasium round the corner, where the Gentiles played naked after the Greek fashion? T. R. Glover put the parents' dilemma humorously: "If we cannot certainly answer the question, Was he allowed to watch the heathen at their athletics? it is easier to answer the question, Did he watch them?"[16]

There can be no doubt about the strict orthodoxy of his parents. Paul was later to describe himself as "a Hebrew born and bred" (or, as the New English Bible puts it, "a Hebrew-speaking Jew of a Hebrew-speaking family"). The context of the phrase gives us the full 'flavour' of his home and upbringing. "Circumcised on my eighth day, Israelite by race, of the tribe of Benjamin, a Hebrew born and bred; in my attitude to the law, a Pharisee; in pious zeal, a persecutor of the church; in legal rectitude, faultless".[17] That gives us a clear indication of the kind of home from which he came. Young Saul learnt early how precious to his parents were the traditions of their fathers – he imbibed them with his mother's milk, he learnt them at her knee, he began to understand their significance at the synagogue services. And there were the periodic visits to Jerusalem. "A man who has not seen the Temple of Herod has not seen a beautiful edifice in his life" – the boy could understand the Rabbis' claim when he saw that "snowy mountain glittering in the sun", as Josephus described it. It was a marvellous structure within an enclosure of something like thirty-five acres. How could he ever forget it, and all that it stood for? "Faith of our fathers, living still . . ."!

Then there was the influence of Gamaliel, whose pupil he was in Jerusalem, and by whom he was "thoroughly trained in every point of our ancestral law".[18] "Held in high regard by all the people",[19] Gamaliel was a grandson of the famous liberal Hillel of whom the story is told that, when a convert asked to be taught the

24

whole law "on one foot", he replied that the entire essence of the Jewish ethic was: "Do not do to your fellow human being what is hurtful to you." Perhaps through the eyes of Gamaliel, Saul got a glimpse of a more tolerant and kindly approach to religion than that which he received in the strict Pharisaism of his parents. If he did, it did nothing to lessen his "boundless devotion to the traditions of my ancestors" in which, according to his own testimony, he "outstripped many of my Jewish contemporaries".[20] It seems that Saul spent a very considerable amount of time in Jerusalem – possibly his parents moved there during his adolescence, the better to shield him from the pagan influences of Tarsus. "I was brought up in this city (Jerusalem)", he was to declare later in his life, and the fact that at that period he had a sister and a nephew living in the city may well point to the family's long association with the centre of Judaism.[21]

To be a Pharisee, as Paul said he was, was to make a proud claim; it was to indicate his sympathy with extreme Jewish orthodoxy. The stern strictures which the Gospels depict Jesus as making against the doctrine and practices of the Pharisees must not blind us to the essential nobility of their movement. *Corruptio optimi pessima.* The movement had begun as a great protest against religious laxity a century and a half before Christ. The Jewish law was being broken, its teachings disobeyed, its practices unheeded under pressure from pagan influence and opposition. The Pharisees were, originally, those who "separated" themselves from such defilement. They held tenaciously to the tradition of their fathers and, often at the cost of their very lives, bore their witness to the teaching of their prophets and wise men. As time went on, there were many of them who spoilt the nobility of their movement by reducing it to a legalistic insistence on observing a complicated code. That was an ever-present danger and, in the light of his later Christian experience, Paul was fully aware of it. The peril of pride, the concept of achieving a righteousness of one's own as a result of good works, is an insidious danger not confined to Pharisaism.

To sum up: we can envisage the tensions which were at work in young Saul, nurtured as he was in the confines of Jewish orthodoxy, stretched by the influence of Hellenic culture and thought-forms. Questions were being raised which would have to be answered, later on.

In addition to all this, there was the matter of his Roman citizenship. If his Jewish name Saul was a constant reminder of Israel's first king and of Saul's inheritance as a member of the tribe of Benjamin, his Roman name Paul reminded him of his status within the Empire. There is no evidence to suggest that he adopted the name Paul at the time of his conversion. From his birth he was a Roman citizen – "I was born free," he replied, with no little pride, to the centurion who otherwise would have had him flogged.[22] He found this citizenship extremely useful. On one occasion, it was enough to elicit an apology from the magistrates at Philippi who, having jailed him and had him publicly flogged, on discovering that he was a Roman citizen freed him and hoped that he would quietly slip away. Not so Paul! "They gave us a public flogging," he said sharply, "though we are Roman citizens and have not been found guilty; they threw us into prison, and are they now to smuggle us out privately? No indeed! Let them come in person and escort us out."[23] And come they did, and escort them out they did! It served Paul well to be a Roman citizen – no further passport was necessary on his travels throughout the world.

But proud as he undoubtedly was of his Roman citizenship, he prized even more his membership of the Jewish race. We have touched on this already, but we must revert to it here and develop it a little. There burned in Paul the fires of a deep and lasting patriotism, a patriotism which was in no sense lessened when, as a Christian, he grasped the universalistic outreach of the Gospel he preached.

The idea of patriotism has for many today uncongenial connotations. One reason is that, all too often, patriotism has been thought of in terms of "my country right or wrong", and to that idea no ethically sensitive person can give allegiance. Another reason, if such it can be called, is that today we are internationalists and we wrongly assume that to be an internationalist means that one cannot be a patriot. Mrs Indira Gandhi resolved that tension rightly when she wrote: "My father . . . declared that no one could be truly international unless he also was intensely national".[24] Father and daughter were right.

The Bible gives us a long series of portraits of people who were intensely patriotic, if by that word we mean people who loved their country dearly and who were convinced of its mission in the purpose of God for his world. Paul was one such. Indeed it was through his passionate patriotism that he came to his universalism – and that without abandoning the former when he was convinced of the latter. If we are to understand that patriotism, we shall do so the better if we glance briefly at some of those men who had gone before him, who belonged to his people and whose blood flowed in his veins.

We see it at its deepest and costliest in such a figure as that of Moses. Aaron had yielded to the pleas of the people and had made them a calf. "These are your gods, O Israel, that brought you up from Egypt." Moses, coming down from the mountain, heard "the sound of singing". Furious, he ground the calf to powder, sprinkled it on water, and made the Israelites drink it. A fearful slaughter of the people followed. Then Moses returned to the Lord: "O hear me! This people has committed a great sin: they have made themselves gods of gold. If thou wilt forgive them, forgive. But if not, blot out my name, I pray, from thy book which thou hast written."[25] That is patriotism – at its best.

Nehemiah was another such patriot. Oppressed by the position of the downtrodden Judaeans and by the desolation of his city of Jerusalem, he determined to take vigorous action and restore their fortunes and their city. But first, before action came prayer, and the opening chapter of the book of Nehemiah shows us the good man mourning, "fasting and praying to the God of heaven". He made no distinction between 'us' and 'them' – he was wholly with them in their plight. "I confess the sins which *we* Israelites have all committed against thee, and of which I and my father's house are also guilty".[26] Daniel, in a somewhat similar situation, provides us with another example of self-identification with his people – "*we* have sinned, *we* have done what was wrong and wicked; *we* have rebelled, *we* have turned our backs on thy commandments and thy decrees. *We* have not listened . . ."[27]

Perhaps the best example of patriotism in the Old Testament is that of Hosea whose story is told in the book which bears his name and whose restless style reflects a passion too deep for orderly expression. His patriotism sprang from the depths and bitterness of his personal and family tragedy, an experience of love spurned and thrown back in his face. Heart-broken, he brooded over his broken marriage, and tried to make sense out of the non-sensical tragedy of Gomer's infidelity. Out of that tragedy, a Gospel began to emerge. His nation was a Gomer, and the heart of his God was broken by her harlotry. "It was one thing to hold in general that God loved Israel; it was another to have that knowledge confirmed by the analogy of his own experience and to know that God *so* loved Israel as Hosea found himself loving Gomer . . ." "Hosea's power was in his wound."[28]

But nowhere in the history of Israel can patriotism, deep and costly, be seen as clearly as it is shown to us in the person of Jesus himself. "O Jerusalem, Jerusalem, the city that murders the prophets and stones the messengers sent to her! How often have I longed to gather your children, as a hen gathers her brood under her wings; but you would not let me." So Luke records.[29] And later: "When he came in sight of the city, he wept

28

over it and said, 'If only you had known, on this great day, the way that leads to peace! But no; it is hidden from your sight.' "[30] The cost of that patriotism was the cross of Calvary.

Moses, Nehemiah, Daniel, Hosea, our Lord himself – it is a noble galaxy of patriots. Paul was the heir of these men. His heart beat in unison with theirs. He knew that the deepest patriotism was a religious patriotism, for only in so far as Israel fulfilled the mission on which she had been sent "to be a light to all peoples"[31] would she be truly great. So far from that being the case, Paul watched her refusing the light for herself and by that refusal inevitably being unable to pass it on to others. Nowhere in his writings does he express his grief more poignantly than in two passages in the Epistle to the Romans: "I am speaking the truth as a Christian, and my own conscience, enlightened by the Holy Spirit, assures me it is no lie: in my heart there is great grief and unceasing sorrow. For I could even pray to be outcast from Christ myself for the sake of my brothers, my natural kinsfolk." (How like this is to Moses' cry, "Blot out my name, I pray, from thy book"!) "They are Israelites: they were made God's sons: theirs is the splendour of the divine presence, theirs the covenants, the law, the temple worship, and the promises. Theirs are the patriarchs, and from them, in natural descent, sprang the Messiah." And a little later: "Brothers, my deepest desire and my prayer to God is for their salvation. To their zeal for God I can testify; but it is an ill-informed zeal. For they ignore God's way of righteousness, and try to set up their own."[32]

With this disastrous story of Israel's rejection of the Messiah Paul wrestles in Romans 9–11. Like his Master, he agonised over the apostasy of Jerusalem. In this matter, as in so many others, he shared in the sufferings of Christ.[33] It was this very patriotism which gave to his missionary work an extra element of urgency – he made it his practice to go first to the synagogues, where he would find the people of his own race at worship, and only then, often after bitter rejection by the Jews, did he go to men of other races.[34] The plan of his missionary strategy is very clearly outlined in the last chapter of the Acts of the Apostles. Paul, under house-arrest, was allowed to call together the Jewish leaders. To them "he spoke urgently of the kingdom of God and sought to convince them about Jesus ..." No agreement was reached. They dispersed, but not before Paul the patriot had remonstrated with them about dulled ears and closed hearts. "Therefore," he concluded, "take notice that this salvation of God has been sent to the Gentiles; the Gentiles will listen."[35] It was a heart-break to the apostle, for his *nation* should have been the "light to lighten the Gentiles". He must take that role on his own shoulders.

And yet, he could not be an ultimate pessimist. He could not believe that God's rejection of his people would be complete. He dared to believe that Israel's numbness of response was temporary, and his spirit reached out to a vision of the reconciliation not only of Israel but of the world. God's purpose was "to show mercy to all mankind".[36] These chapters in Romans (9–11) end with a doxology of hope: "O depth of wealth, wisdom, and knowledge in God! How unsearchable his judgements, how untraceable his ways! . . . Source, Guide, and Goal of all that is – to him be glory for ever! Amen."[37]

From the deeps of his own religious patriotism, Paul came through to a larger vision, a supra-nationalism, adumbrated by Old Testament seers and now beginning to be realised in the Church, a new humanity, the consummation of God's plan, when Christ shall reign, "all enemies under his feet", even the Son himself being made "subordinate to God who made all things subject to him, and thus God will be all in all".[38]

But those convictions, that missionary task, lay in days yet future in the experience of this man of two worlds.

2

NEW CREATION

Saul was such an obstinate creature that it was necessary for God to seize him by the scruff of his neck and fling him to the ground and strike him blind before he would turn towards the light. And even then it took him many years before the light permeated the whole of his being and he could be described as truly enlightened.

Donald Nicholl: *Holiness*

> Saint Paul is often criticised
> By modern people who're annoyed
> At his conversion, saying Freud
> Explains it all. But they omit
> The really vital point of it,
> Which isn't *how* it was achieved
> But what it was that Paul believed.

John Betjeman

God crosses through the thickness of the world to come to us.

Simone Weil: *Gravity and Grace*

> Through such souls alone
> God stooping shows sufficient of his light
> For us i' the dark to rise by.
> And I rise.

Robert Browning: *Rabbi ben Ezra*

2

NEW CREATION

The conversion of Paul has very frequently been taken as the classic example of sudden and dramatic spiritual change. Indeed, in some circles it has almost been assumed that unless, to a lesser or greater degree, there has been some parallel to such an alleged and dateable event, a measure of doubt must be cast on the reality of a man's religious discipleship. It is, therefore, a matter of some importance to look closely at the conversion of which – rightly – theologians and artists have made so much in the course of subsequent history.

"Sudden and dramatic spiritual change." We may certainly use the word "dramatic" of the events of the story told thrice in the Acts of the Apostles[1] and referred to, obliquely, by Paul several times in his letters. But a very large question-mark should be placed against the description "sudden". There are many factors which indicate that there had been a considerable period before the great event, during which there was a build-up of inflammable material which needed only the divine spark on the Damascus road to set it alight. Let us look at some of this material.

There must always be an element of doubt about the first factor, but it is of such importance that it must at least be considered. It revolves around the question: had Saul seen Jesus? There are those who categorically dismiss the question and deny the possibility. I cannot be among their number. We are not certain of the exact chronology of the life of Jesus nor indeed of Paul. But we know enough of both to make it appear more than likely that they were contemporaries pretty close in age to one another. We know that Jesus had a ministry in Jerusalem – the Fourth Gospel would indicate that that southern ministry was longer than a reading of the Synoptic Gospels would suggest (though even in them there are hints of such a ministry: "O Jerusalem, Jerusalem . . . *How often* have I longed to gather your children, as a hen gathers her brood under her wings; but you would not let me.")[2] There were undoubtedly visits paid by our Lord to the capital, including preaching and teaching visits, between that first memorable journey as a boy of twelve which Luke records[3] and the final visit for the passion and crucifixion.

We need not doubt that young Saul of Tarsus, son as he was of devout Jewish parents, would also have visited the Temple at Jerusalem probably several times before he went there to undertake serious study at the feet of Gamaliel – study which may have involved him in some years of residence. Put these two series of probabilities together, and is it not possible, indeed highly likely, that the young teacher from Galilee and the young Pharisee from Tarsus would have looked into one another's eyes, and that Saul would have heard Jesus teach? And who could so see and hear without some deep impression being made? That the impression may have elicited resistance is, at the moment, neither here nor there. The important point is that an impression was probably made on Saul at an age when such impressions go deep and have about them an element of permanence.

Then there was Stephen, the story of whose stoning is told in the Acts, with the significant footnote added to it: "Saul was among those who approved of his murder."[4] Stephen is mentioned to us as one of a group of men who were set apart by the early Church to deal with certain matters of administration which were calling for attention. It soon became clear that, in the case of Stephen, the brief was too restrictive – he was a man endowed with gifts of spiritual leadership. He is described as "a man full of faith and of the Holy Spirit . . . full of grace and power", whose face was "like the face of an angel" as he rose to answer the charge made against him by the Jewish Council, the Sanhedrin.[5] His address "touched" his hearers "on the raw and they ground their teeth with fury . . . They made one rush at him, and, flinging him out of the city, set about stoning him."[6]

There was nothing pretty about death by stoning. "The victim was made to stand on a wall about ten or fifteen feet high, completely naked. The first 'witness' knocked him off it. If the fall did not kill him, then the second 'witness' dropped a stone on his chest. If he still remained alive, the bystanders finished him off with other stones."[7] It was strenuous work stoning a man. You had to take your coat off to do it. "The witnesses laid their coats at the feet of a young man named Saul." "He approved" – approved? Yes; how could he do otherwise, he, a Pharisee looking for the coming Messiah, and listening to Stephen witnessing to a Messiah already come, now standing at God's right hand ready to aid him? How could he do other than approve his death when the man started praying to the Lord Jesus and – worst of all – prayed for his murderers, just as his Lord had done? Another impression, deep and permanent, was made on Saul that terrible day.

Then there were the groups whom Saul harried. Saul the Pharisee had become Saul the inquisitor. He got himself letters from the High Priest which authorised him to go so far as to arrest anyone he found, man or woman, in the synagogues at Damascus who followed the new Way, and to bring them to Jerusalem.[8] Questions inevitably precede arrests, and questions evoke answers. Saul learned much during those hours of questioning – and not only about the life and teaching of Jesus who had captured these followers of the Way, but also about the men and women themselves. They seemed to have a quality of life, a serenity under persecution, an undergirding joy which spoke more eloquently than their sometimes hesitant words. They did not need to say much about love – they were living the life of love. There was an authenticity about them which pierced him. His deep animosity was excited, but at the same time he found himself fascinated by the sheer beauty of lives transformed.

So it all built up – the eyes and voice of Jesus himself (probably); the face of Stephen (how often that face haunted Saul in the hours of the night when he could not sleep but heard again the prayer, "Lord, do not hold this sin against them"!); the faces and voices, the serene personalities, of those whom he persecuted. It was maddening – all so stupid – the antithesis of what he had been taught. He must oppose it, root and branch. He must ravage this infant Church. No matter if his hands were stained with their blood. His cause was righteous. "I once thought it my duty to oppose with the utmost vigour the name of Jesus of Nazareth. Yes, that is what I did in Jerusalem, and I had many of God's people imprisoned on the authority of the chief priests, and when they were on trial for their lives I gave my vote against them. Many and many a time in all the synagogues I had them punished and I used to try and force them to deny their Lord. I was mad with fury against them, and I hounded them to distant cities."[9] "You have heard", he was to write a few years later to some friends, ". . . how savagely I persecuted the church of God, and tried to destroy it."[10]

And then it happened. Let us not ask, too precisely, what 'it' was. We may use psychological jargon if we will; it may help, it may not. We may posit the possibility that Saul had an epileptic fit. That may help some; it does not help me. Rather, let us beware the banality of seeking to explain the ways of God with men, the God who has as many ways of reaching our innermost beings with his love as he has of giving us different faces or different finger-prints. When God touches a man, turns him round in his tracks, looks into the eyes of the one who hitherto has been running away from him and crucifying the Son of God afresh, let us not try to explain that miracle of love and grace. Let us remember that, as there is a mystery surrounding the Being of God, so there is a mystery at the heart of his ways with men. Perhaps above every story of conversion we should write the warning: "Mystery! God at work!"

If we want to pursue the mystery – and the pursuit, if undertaken with awe, is abundantly worthwhile – we shall find most help in asking how the man concerned saw it all. No doubt, his own language will prove incapable of bearing the weight of the miracle which it seeks to describe. But it is likely that, if he will let us look through his eyes, we shall see it more accurately than through the eyes of any other. And he has not left us without a good deal to go on.

The three accounts of the events on the Damascus road given in the Acts of the Apostles doubtless owe their origin to Paul himself, though they have come to us through the agency of Luke. Though they differ in certain details, they are at one in their story of a brilliant light, and of the voice of *enquiry* ("Saul, Saul, why do you persecute me?"), of *revelation* ("I am Jesus, whom you are persecuting"), and of *command* ("get up and go . . . I send you").

In Paul's letters, while we do not get another record of the events of that great day, we have several passages which indicate very clearly what the experience on the Damascus road meant to him. We shall look at four of these:

(i) In writing to the Corinthians about the ministry of proclamation, he used the plural "we", but it is quite clear that he had in mind primarily his own ministry based, as it was, on his own experience of God in Christ. "It is not ourselves that we proclaim; we proclaim Christ Jesus as Lord, and ourselves as your servants, for Jesus' sake. For the same God who said, 'Out of darkness let light shine', has caused his light to shine within us, to give the light of revelation – the revelation of the glory of God in the face of Jesus Christ."[11] Clearly, Paul was here looking back to the experience on the Damascus road. Equally clearly, he was interpreting it in terms of the creation story of the first chapter of Genesis. The writer there depicts a scene of primeval chaos – "the earth was without form and void". God spoke; there was order. "Darkness was over the face of the abyss". God spoke: there was light.[12] It was a perfect description of Paul's own experience, before God touched him, and after. Chaos and darkness – how well he remembered it! The resistance he had put up against the evidence he saw in Stephen and in the disciples of Jesus; the savagery with which he had ravaged the Church; the sleepless nights when the battle raged in his own soul – "chaos and darkness" described it all too well. Then God spoke: "Saul, Saul, why . . .? You are hurting *yourself* by kicking against the goads", and there was *order*. Those had been dark days – and even darker nights – since Stephen had died. Would the darkness never lift? Then God spoke, and there was *light*, light so blinding that it left him, temporarily, physically blind.

This was, indeed, a new creation. Speaking out of a deep experience of his own, he wrote: "When anyone is united to Christ, there is a new world (or, a new act of creation); the old order has gone, and a new order has already begun."[13] Moffatt's translation gets the point well: "There is a new creation whenever a man comes to be in Christ". In his own person, the miracle of creation had taken place all over again. And God looked down and saw it all – "and God saw that it was good", very good, a man being re-created.

(ii) Even more intimately and personally, Paul wrote in another passage of being "taken hold of" by Christ – "hoping to take hold of that for which Christ once took hold of me";[14] "grasping ever more firmly the purpose for which Christ Jesus grasped me".[15] There is something wonderfully integrating in that grasp of Christ. To know that one is so held is to be guarded against the dissipation of one's energies and powers. "*This one thing* I do," he wrote in this same passage.[16] "I lost

38

myself among a multiplicity of things," Augustine wrote of his pre-conversion days.[17] Paul might have said the same of his. Then Christ grasped him with a *constraining* love, as he said elsewhere – "the love of Christ holds us within bounds, controls us".[18] This was not the narrowing of his vision or the limiting of his powers or the diminution of his personality. It was the very reverse. "Whatever constricts a man strengthens him" – so André Gide makes Joseph de Maistre remark.[19] The motto of a London theological College puts it succinctly: "*Et teneo et teneor*" – "I hold and I am held." That is fulfilment.

(iii) Can one doubt that behind such a passage as the following lies the experience of the man who wrote it: God "ordained that" his own "should be shaped to the likeness of his Son"?[20] The passage is a deeply theological one, but it could not have been written except by one who realised that that 'shaping' process was going on in his own character. The metaphor sounds like that of the potter at work at his wheel, fashioning a vessel which would in some measure reflect the beauty of its creator. The process had begun on the Damascus road, in Paul's case. It would never end, till the likeness of the Son of God could be seen even in him – the miracle of the new creation was a continuing one.

(iv) If Paul's own experience lies behind the potter-metaphor in Romans 8, it surely also lies behind the longer and more elaborate passage in Romans 7: 7–25. It may well be that the oft-repeated "I" in these verses is a stylistic way of enunciating the experience of any conscientious person faced with the "thou shalt" of the law, on the one hand, and with his own moral weakness, on the other. But as I read the passage, I am aware of an agony, a struggle, a defeat which is severely personal. Here is the experience of the lusty boy untroubled by law – "there was a time when, in the absence of law, I was fully alive". Then came the consciousness of law, and "sin sprang to life and I died" (v.9). The death-knell may be universal in its application, but in this passage there is something terribly autobiographical about it. Paul had made a "discovery" – that "when I want to do the right, only the wrong is within my reach" (v.21). But – and here is the key to the glory of his gospel – he had also made the discovery that there is "rescue ... through Jesus Christ our Lord! Thanks be to God!" (vv.24–25).

We cannot analyse with any clinical exactitude the ways of God with men. They baffle analysis. We cannot explain them any more than we can explain the glory of a sunset or the miracle of a rose-bud. We can only observe – and thank – and worship. We can listen to those who have had dealings with God – and wonder and adore. After all, Paul was only one of a multitude over the centuries to whom God has come and whom he has touched on the shoulder, called by name, and sent on his errands. No matter whether the coming has been dramatic, or slow and silent as the rising dawn. What matters is that there has been meeting – and response – and sending – and awe – and worship. The point is of major importance, and is worth illustrating.

Listen to Augustine writing of his conversion. Like Paul's, it was the result of a long process in which tension, desire and self-loathing all had a part. Callously he had sent away his mistress with whom he had lived for fifteen years, and kept their son, Adeodatus, whom he dearly loved. For long he had wrestled with his doubts and his temptations, while Monica his mother prayed on. Then, one day, in the garden of his house in Milan,

I heard a voice from some nearby house, a boy's voice or a girl's voice, I do not know: but it was a sort of sing-song repeated again and again, "Take and read, take and read". I ceased weeping and immediately began to search my mind most carefully as to whether children were accustomed to chant these words in any kind of game, and I could not remember that I had ever heard any such thing. Damming back the flood of my tears I arose, interpreting the incident as quite certainly a divine command to open my book of Scripture and read the passage at which I should open. . . . I snatched it up, opened it and in silence read the passage upon which my eyes first fell: *Not in rioting and drunkenness, not in chambering and impurities, not in contention and envy, but put ye on the Lord Jesus Christ and make not provision for the flesh in its concupiscences* (Romans 13: 13). I had no wish to read further, and no need. For in that instant, with the very ending of the sentence, it was as though a light of utter confidence shone in my heart, and all the darkness of uncertainty vanished away. . . . Then we [his friend Alypius and himself] went in to my mother and told her, to her great joy. We related how it had come about: she was filled with triumphant exultation, and praised you who are mighty beyond what we ask or conceive.[21]

Augustine became Bishop of Hippo in North Africa.

Confronted with the dissolution of the Roman Empire, like a latter-day Noah, he was constrained to construct an ark, in his case Orthodoxy, wherein his Church could survive through the dark days that lay ahead. Thanks largely to Augustine, the light of the New Testament did not go out with Rome's but remained amidst the debris of the fallen empire to light the way to another civilisation, Christendom, whose legatees we are.

So, finely, Malcolm Muggeridge comments.[22]

Listen to Thomas Merton. His book, *The Seven Storey Mountain*, is a moving piece of spiritual autobiography. He was always to look back on his time at Cambridge with a kind of horror and yet in retrospect he was thankful, for "God in his mercy was permitting me to fly as far as I could from his love but at the same time preparing to confront me, at the end of it all, and in the

41

bottom of the abyss, when I thought I had gone farthest away from him."[23] It was a kind of descent into hell with resurrection to follow. There came a time when "I began to want to take the necessary means to achieve this union, this peace. I began to desire to dedicate my life to God, to his service." He began to realise that the intellect is constantly being blinded and perverted by the ends and aims of passion, and

> we have become marvellous at self-delusion. . . . There are ways that seem to men to be good, the end whereof is in the depths of hell. The only answer to the problem is grace, grace, docility to grace.
>
> Finally the urge [towards the Catholic Church] became so strong that I could not resist it. I called up my girl and told her that I was not coming out that weekend, and made up my mind to go to Mass for the first time in my life . . . I will not easily forget how I felt that day. First, there was this sweet, strong, gentle, clean urge in me which said: "Go to Mass! Go to Mass!" . . . It had a suavity, a simplicity about it that I could not easily account for. And when I gave in to it, it did not exult over me, and trample me down in its raging haste to land on its prey, but it carried me forward serenely and with purposeful direction.

He went to Mass.

> God made it a very beautiful Sunday. And since it was the first time I had ever really spent a sober Sunday in New York, I was surprised at the clean, quiet atmosphere of the empty streets up-town. The sun was blazing bright. At the end of the street, as I came out the front door, I could see a burst of green, and the blue river and the hills of Jersey on the other side.[24]

Paul and Thomas Merton were very different personalities, but they both experienced the "glory of the lighted mind"[25] when Christ laid hold of them.

Gerald Priestland, in one of the last of his memorable Saturday morning talks in the *Yours Faithfully* series, quoted from a letter which he had received from a Cornish mining engineer. He wrote: "I am no plaster saint. I live very much in the world. But what I have told you now is the first time I have ever told anybody." He went on to tell of how it happened thirty-four years ago:

I suppose I had nodded off. For I woke up with the sun streaming down on my face – just enjoying doing nothing in particular, listening to the birds singing. Suddenly, I became aware of a strange mixture of fear and uplift entering my mind, and sat there deeply puzzled for some minutes. Finally, it became so insistent that I had to find out what it meant.

I walked up the passage to my bedroom, went down on my knees, and asked. As I did so, the glory of the universe shone before me. I was blinded by the dazzling bright light. In my heart, I flung my arms before my eyes, because I knew that man could not look upon God and live. I was both terrified and yet up-lifted – I can't explain it – I was shattered. And then I knew that I was a nothing. All my conceit and personal esteem vanished.

So great and awful was the holiness that stood before me that I feared lest it should ever happen again. But it completely changed my life. When I hear men in their folly say, "You can't prove that there is a God," I reply, "You wait until he takes half a step towards you, and you are left in no doubt."[26]

We have listened to the witness of three men who, like Paul, found their darkness turned to light, their chaos to order. Let us listen to but one more – Leo Tolstoy. The man who wrote about his earlier life: "I knew not what I wanted, I was afraid of life, I shrank from it and yet there was something I hoped for from it," wrote in unforgettable words about his conversion: "Five years ago I came to believe in Christ's teaching,

43

and my life suddenly changed; I ceased to desire what I had previously desired, and began to desire what I formerly did not want. What had previously seemed to me good seemed evil, and what had seemed evil seemed good."[27]

God is very patient, very gentle, very persistent. Paul and Augustine and Thomas Merton and Gerald Priestland's unknown correspondent and Leo Tolstoy would all agree. And so does the witness of "the Holy Church throughout all the world".

Let us listen, finally, to part of one of Francis Thompson's finest poems, for the poets often pierce nearer to the heart of things than do the rest of us. Most of those whom we have just been considering could have echoed the words with which he begins his poem *The Hound of Heaven*:

I fled him, down the nights and down the days:
I fled him, down the arches of the years;
I fled him, down the labyrinthine ways
    Of my own mind; and in the mist of tears
I hid from him, and under running laughter.
        Up vistaed hopes I sped;
        And shot, precipitated,
Adown Titanic glooms of chasmed fears,
    from those strong Feet that followed, followed after.
        But with unhurrying chase,
        And unperturbèd pace,
Deliberate speed, majestic instancy,
        They beat – and a Voice beat
        More instant than the Feet –
"All things betray thee, who betrayest me."

He ends his poem thus:

Halts by me that footfall:
Is my gloom, after all,
Shade of his hand, outstretched caressingly?
"Ah, fondest, blindest, weakest,

44

I am he whom thou seekest!
Thou dravest love from thee, who dravest me."

For Paul, the change that occurred at his conversion was indeed dramatic, though not so sudden as many have thought it to have been. God's ways with men are manifold, and often lacking in the sudden or the dramatic. It is a quiet "footfall" that "halts by" them, and the "shade of his hand" can easily be mistaken. It is a moment of supreme importance when response is made, for then man begins to realise his destiny as a human being – "man dwells at that point of the universe, poised between the pull of the earthly and the heavenly, where God can cross over and reach him and render unto him grace." At that point, life begins.

What happened to Paul that day on the Damascus road was more than a revolution within him. It was a revelation also of what God was to do through him in the years ahead. The accounts in the Acts differ as to how that revelation was made to him. The first two accounts simply indicate that he was told to get up from the ground on to which he had fallen when the light blazed out, and go into the city of Damascus; he would then be told what he had to do. The third account elaborates the purpose for which the divine presence had appeared to him – "I have appeared to you for a purpose: to appoint you my servant and witness, to testify . . . to open [the Gentiles'] eyes and turn them from darkness to light, from the dominion of Satan to God."[28] Perhaps Paul, looking back over the years in which his ministry had developed, was reading more into his original call than what actually came to him that day. Suffice it to say that, when the light shone and the voice spoke, the seed of mission was sown in Paul's heart. This revelation was not for himself alone; there was a world awaiting it. Grollenberg puts it vividly: "Paul the Jew died near Damascus. At the same time he became a new creation, a new man, along with all those other unworthy people who had become involved with the Messiah, God's

Christ. In his unimaginable love, Jesus had opened a new way for all men, for those countless people who did not deserve it, including the Gentiles."[29]

"The *seed* of mission", we said. A tiny seed is a mighty thing. It has within it the power to lift a pavement, or unsettle a foundation. The seed sown in Paul's heart and mind that day had within it the power to change a world. The man to whom the revelation had been given, the man in whom the revolution had taken place, was himself to be a revolutionary entrusted with a global Gospel.

FRUITFUL DESERT

We shall never be safe in the market-place unless we
are at home in the desert.

Basil Hume: *Searching for God*

After the fire the breath of a light whisper.

I Kings 19: 12 (Moffatt)

Great things are done when men and mountains meet;
This is not done by jostling in the street.

William Blake: *Gnomic Verses*

Come now, little man, put aside your business for a
while, take refuge for a little from your tumultuous
thoughts, cast off your cares and let your burdensome
distractions wait. Take some leisure for God. Rest
awhile in him. Enter into the chamber of your mind –
put out everything except God and whatever helps you
to seek him, close your door and seek him.

Say now to God, with all your heart, "I seek thy face,
O God, thy face I seek."

Anselm, Archbishop of Canterbury (*c*.1033–1109)

3

FRUITFUL DESERT

A seed needs time to germinate and grow. Paul needed time to think – to pray – to plan. The revelation on the Damascus road had shattered him. Gone were his pride, his confidence in his achievements, the assurance of his moral rightness. God's love had broken all that down. But how was he to face the future?

The voice had said: "Continue your journey to Damascus; there you will be told of all the tasks that are laid upon you."[1] One step at a time – that was a sound direction. So to Damascus he went. God had his man in readiness, just at the point when Paul needed such a man. The story of Ananias as Luke tells it is full of insight into human character and divine grace. In him we see a man very diffident about the conviction that came to him that he must meet Paul and minister to him. We may call him a coward, if we will; but first we should ask how we ourselves would have reacted if the command had come to us to go at once to a certain house and ask for the man who had been responsible for the deaths of our colleagues! "Lord, I have often heard about this man . . ." Indeed he had. "But the Lord said to him, 'You must go . . . '"[2] And go he did, even if his knees shook as he knocked at the door of the house where Paul was lodged with one, Judas.

Then a lovely thing happened. Grace took over. "Saul, *my brother*", he said, and, not content with words, he "laid his hands on him". Touch, in difficult moments, can often say more than words. In this case, there were both words and touch. And Paul found himself welcomed into the brotherhood of the Church, though there were to be others, a little later, who were afraid to welcome him, till Barnabas "took him by the hand" (the touch again!) "and introduced him to the apostles".[3] As J. A. Hutton put it well – Ananias offered him "in the name of Christ, the freedom of the new city of God!"[4]

What happened after the meeting with Ananias? His sight restored, Paul "was baptised, and afterwards he took food and his strength returned". Physical health followed spiritual regeneration. But what then? The record in Acts 9 says that "he stayed some time with the disciples in Damascus. Soon he was proclaiming Jesus publicly in the synagogues ... Saul grew more and more forceful, and silenced the Jews of Damascus with his cogent proofs that Jesus was the Messiah."[5] The account is so written as to indicate that the events in this series followed rapidly one after the other.

But, in an autobiographical passage in the Epistle to the Galatians, Paul says that, after God's revelation of his Son to him, "without consulting any human being, without going up to Jerusalem to see those who were apostles before me, *I went off at once to Arabia*, and afterwards returned to Damascus."[6] It is difficult to reconcile the two accounts and to make them fit chronologically. Paul in his letter to the Galatians is at pains to make the point that his commission came direct from God and needed no corroboration from men, apostles or anybody else. Arabia, not headquarters at Jerusalem, was the place to go after the great conversion experience. If we must seek to reconcile the two stories, we can only suppose that after a brief period of evangelistic activity in Damascus, he went off to Arabia – but "went off at once" is difficult.

The importance of the apostle's time in Arabia must not be underestimated. By 'Arabia' he presumably meant the extensive kingdom of the Nabataeans which stretched from Damascus across Transjordan and present-day Saudi Arabia. Its capital, Petra, the "rose-red city half as old as time", lay some fifty-five miles south of the Dead Sea and about the same distance north of the Gulf of Aqaba. Standing in a basin-like valley, protected on all sides by steep and rocky mountains, the city's only access was, and still is, a dark and winding cleft which the water has worn through the rock over the centuries. We should think of Paul, then, as spending his time in a rough, rocky, hot area, mostly deserted by human beings, but by no means wholly so, for there would have been nomadic tribes in the vicinity and the desert was criss-crossed by caravan routes operating between Arabia and Egypt. Both these points are to be noted – the loneliness of the area, *and*, in parts and at times, the presence of people in considerable numbers.

Much has been written as to Paul's reason for going off to Arabia. There are those who believe that he went there to be alone with God. There are those who believe that he went on an evangelistic errand. The answer need not necessarily be seen in terms of either-or. We can think of him engaging in both activities, successively.

Whether or not this journey was taken after a brief period of evangelistic activity in Damascus, I believe that, soon after his conversion, Paul felt the imperative need of being alone with God. The long build-up of events which led to his conversion had been a period of severe tension, the results of which were only fully felt when the tension gave way to peace and integration. After God's loving hammer-blow had struck him to the ground, he arose dazed and blind. Ananias had been a healing influence, Paul's baptism a benediction. But there was a new world awaiting discovery, and no one, at that moment, could help him undertake it. This Jesus whom he had persecuted he now saw to be the Christ, the Son of God. That immense revelation had to be 'digested', and the process would take time. The Gospel which the followers of Jesus had tremblingly tried to outline to their inquisitor had now to be pieced together and its significance assessed. Could it be that the message of the Gospel was not for the Jews only but was also of universal application?[7] If so, the whole idea of election would have to be re-thought – not in terms of privilege but of responsibility. Could it really be that in the eyes of God it was immaterial whether a man was Jew or Gentile, slave or free? And was it possible that sex distinctions no longer obtained, and that in Christ male and female were one? The questions kept pouring into his fertile mind. If these ideas were true, if Jesus was the way, the truth, the life, then in his immediate surroundings there were men and women who should be told. And in the synagogues where the Scriptures were regularly read, the Jews should hear: for example, those passages in Isaiah about the suffering Servant,[8] did they not take on an entirely new meaning since those events on a hill outside Jerusalem only a very few years ago? And the circles of Gentile 'God-fearers', who wistfully listened in to the reading of the Jewish Scriptures at the synagogue services, and who longed for a religion and an ethic which the effete religions of their world had failed to give them – should not they also be told? And what of the people in his own home city of Tarsus – his parents, his university friends, his colleagues in the synagogue? His mind ranged out – to Philippi and Ephesus, to Athens, yes and to Rome, the hub of the universe. Did Christ die for the people of these cities as well as for the men of the caravans passing through Arabia? Paul must have time. He must have quiet. He must talk it out with God. The significance of the revolution within him must be assessed if he was to become a positive revolutionary.

The desert has always been a fruitful place in the making of men of God. Elijah, exhausted by his encounter with the prophets of Baal and fearful for his life, fled to Beersheba and then, leaving his servant there, "went a day's journey into the wilderness". It was there that he found the physical refreshment that he so sorely needed. It was there that he heard "the sound of a gentle stillness", and was able to face the penetrating question that God asked him: "Why are you here, Elijah?"[9]

Amos's training to be a prophet – the last thing he ever dreamed of! – took place in the years of his youth as he tended the sheep and the goats and gathered the fruit from the wild-fig shrubs. Tekoa, whence he came, was a lonely place, quiet enough for him to hear the Lord saying to him, "Go and prophesy to my people Israel."[10]

"John the Baptist appeared in the wilderness . . . and they flocked to him."[11]

Jesus – "the Spirit sent him away into the wilderness, and there he remained for forty days . . ."[12]

Helen Waddell, in her classic book *The Desert Fathers*,[13] introduces us to something of the power of the desert life. We may shrink from the extremes of austerity to which some of these men went, but we should remind ourselves that 'asceticism' comes from a Greek word *askēsis* which simply means 'training'. Miss Waddell's book shows us how men became God's athletes until, after long years of withdrawal and listening, they found that people flocked to them, with their sins and their problems, as men would flock to a spring after long periods of drought.

Henri J. M. Nouwen's book, *The Way of the Heart: Desert Spirituality and Contemporary Ministry*, is largely a protest against our wordiness and a plea for silence. He tells a pointed story: "One day Archbishop Theophilus came to the desert to visit Abba Pambo. But Abba Pambo did not speak to him. When the brethren finally said to Pambo, 'Father, say something to the archbishop, so that he may be edified,' he replied: 'If he is not edified by my silence, he will not be edified by my speech.'"[14]

If ever there was a man of words, it was Thomas Merton. He wrote prolifically and his books are printed and read throughout the world. But there were times when words wearied him. He wrote: "How weary I am of being a writer. How necessary it is for monks to work in the fields, in the rain, in the sun, in the mud, in the clay, in the wind: these are our spiritual directors and our novice-masters. They form our contemplation. They instil us with virtue. They make us as stable as the land we live in. You do not get that out of a type-writer."[15] And in his autobiography he tells how, looking out from his room at St Bonaventure's college, "my eyes often . . . rested in that peaceful scene, and the landscape became associated with my prayers . . . As the months went on, I began to drink poems out of those hills."[16] We may ask: did not Paul drink his great poem to love, which he gave us in the thirteenth chapter of I Corinthians, out of the open spaces of Arabia?

Paul *needed* the desert, the rain, the sun, the mud, the clay, the wind, the sand, if he was to sort things out and begin to catch the meaning of the words that came to him on the Damascus road – "I am Jesus". He needed the desert if he was to be "fashioned after the likeness of God's Son". And he needed the desert, needed to be away from men, if he was to become the sort of man to whom people would come in their need. Benoit Charlemagne, a member of the Capuchin order, tells of one such, Hubert, who came to live in a tumbledown house near Aix-en-Provence.

> This old man, once priest of an important parish, a kind of giant radiating a sense of security and the joy of life, had suddenly decided to live quite alone as a hermit, in order to pray to God. But very quickly his numerous friends had discovered his retreat and come to visit him. Then more and more drop-outs, hoodlums, slumdwellers, and vagabonds had come to settle themselves in his bedroom, in his kitchen and even in his chapel. They were all young people, alone and embittered, who had run away from their families or come out of prison; some of them were drug addicts, one was a deserter. That is still going on today.[17]

Would they have come, if Hubert had not first learnt the meaning of being alone with God? The communion in the desert comes before the activity of ministry.

Often, in his synagogue worship, Saul of Tarsus must have noticed how much stress the psalmists and prophets laid on waiting on God. Their hope in God, their expectancy of his gracious activity and rescuing power, derived from the attitude of *waiting*. "I waited, waited for the Lord, he bent down to me and heard my cry."[18] "I wait for the Lord with all my soul, I hope for the fulfilment of his word. My soul waits for the Lord more eagerly than watchmen for the morning. Like men who watch for the morning, O Israel, look for the Lord."[19] "Young men may grow weary and faint . . . but those who look to the Lord (they that wait upon the Lord – AV) will win new strength."[20]

This was one of the deepest notes of Israel's spirituality. Saul had given intellectual assent to it, even begun to appreciate its importance in his pre-conversion days. But now he saw the utter necessity of entering deeply into its meaning, of waiting in steady reliance on God, of eagerly looking into his face for guidance, strength, refreshment. He worked it out, in a new depth of understanding, in Arabia.

That period in the desert was for Paul a period of dialogue with his Lord. He could not have done what he did had there not been those months in Arabia, getting clear the dimensions of God's plan for his world, envisaging his part in the fulfilment of that plan, a time of prayer, worship and communion. In Arabia, Paul was in the making. The missionary was emerging.

> Through men whom worldlings count as fools
> Chosen of God and not of man,
> Rear'd in thy sacred training schools,
> Goes forward thine eternal plan.

Arabia was God's "sacred training school" for Paul. That was the primary purpose of his being there and of his remaining there for three years, as he tells us in the letter to the Galatians[21] (though, by the ancient habit of inclusive reckoning, the "three years later" may mean two years). The outline of a strategy was beginning to emerge – there was Damascus, near which it had all begun; and Tarsus, the place of his family and birth; and Philippi, "the little Rome away from Rome," where the famous road to the west, the Via Egnatia, began; and Ephesus, the centre of idol worship with all its obscenities; and Rome, the heart of the Empire; and Spain, "the pillars of Hercules", the utmost limits of the world in the west.

That would need thinking out – a larger strategy. Meanwhile, and nearer home, there were opportunities for evangelism waiting to be seized. There was Petra itself, the residence of the Nabataean King Aretas IV (whose commissioner was to prove very unfriendly to the apostle).[22] There were Gerasa and Philadelphia (the modern Amman). There were many Jewish inhabitants in these and similar towns. And there were the caravans plying their trade. Touch these men on their errands and who could say where they might take the Gospel, more precious than any of their wares and to be received "without money and without price"? St Chrysostom and many of the fathers interpreted Paul's withdrawal into Arabia as a mission for the conversion of the Arabs. James Stewart describes that as "rather curious exegesis".[23] But we need not so regard it. That it was secondary in importance to the purpose of Paul's being alone with God there can be no doubt. But it is highly probable that it was a natural outcome of that aloneness and of that dialogue.

As he pondered, the fires burned –

Oh could I tell, ye surely would believe it!
Oh could I only say what I have seen!
How should I tell or how can ye receive it,
How, till he bringeth you where I have been?[24]

Conviction turned to passion in Arabia – a passion which burned the fiercer for Paul's belief in the imminence of the return of Christ. Time was short. He must share the treasure of his new-found faith.

Arabia, with its large areas of solitude, was ideal for quiet, for thought, for prayer, for dialogue with God, for the forming of a strategy. Arabia, with its centres of population and with the men of the caravans, was no less ideal for the beginnings of his missionary work.

It was a fruitful desert.

4

A CHARACTER

We are only human beings, no less mortal than you.

Acts 14: 15 (NEB)

We are only human beings with feelings just like yours!

ibid. (Phillips)

I verily thought with myself, that I ought to do many things contrary to the name of Jesus of Nazareth.

Acts 26: 9 (AV)

This one thing I do . . . I press toward the mark for the prize . . .

Philippians 3: 13–14 (AV)

4

A CHARACTER

What manner of man was this Paul? Cathedrals have
been named after him; his effigy has been carved on
countless buildings and depicted in thousands of
stained-glass windows; his writings have changed the
course of history, and enchanted, enriched, and enraged
thinkers over the centuries. Is it possible to go behind
the accretions of the years and, as it were, to strip the
halo with which artists have adorned him? The prefac-
ing of his name by the title 'Saint' has, like the halo,
tended to separate him from the ordinary run of humanity. Was he a man who lived above the level of temptations which assail ordinary mortals, or was he attacked
and, sometimes, overcome by them? If we had run
across him in Jerusalem, had a drink with him in
Ephesus, or spent an evening with him in Rome, what
sort of man should we have met? Should we have been
put off by the encounter, and hope never to meet him
again? Or should we have been warmed and sent on our
way encouraged?

To find some answer to these questions is of great
importance, for unless we can catch a glimpse of the face
behind the letters which he wrote we shall not be able to
understand them. In fact, those letters and the very
large section of the Acts of the Apostles which is devoted
to his life and work provide us with a pretty clear
picture of the character of the apostle.

But first, a word about the chronology of his life. We
do not know the exact date of his birth. If we put it
roughly at the beginning of the first century, we shall
not be far out.[1] Stewart Perowne estimates that he was
"about thirty years of age", when, as Saul of Tarsus, he

"intervened in the critical affairs of Jerusalem Jewry".[2] We may put his conversion about the year AD 33. Moving to the end of his life and ministry, we can affirm with confidence that he reached Rome early in AD 60, there to begin a two-year period of detention. Whether he fulfilled his desire of going to Spain[3] history does not record, nor does it give us the exact date of his death. That is generally put at about AD 65 in Rome.

We see, then, that the Christian ministry of the apostle was exercised over a period of about three decades – years of intense activity, extensive travel, astonishing success, deep suffering, ultimate martyrdom.

Of his physical appearance we have an early description that is sufficiently unflattering to have about it a ring of truth. *The Acts of Paul and Thekla* which, Sir William Ramsay believed, went "back ultimately to a document of the first century" though enlarged and revised about AD 130,[4] gives us this picture of the apostle: "A man of moderate stature, with curly hair and scanty, crooked legs, with blue eyes and large knit eyebrows, long nose, and he was full of the grace and pity of the Lord, sometimes having the appearance of a man, and sometimes looking like an angel." Other versions of the text vary in detail, but the overall picture remains much the same. Paul himself was honest enough to report what some of his Corinthian correspondents said about him – "he has no presence, and as a speaker he is beneath contempt"[5] (a description, we may suspect, which tells us more about the Corinthians than it does about Paul!). But we may guess from these descriptions that his leadership derived from something deeper and more subtle than excellence of physique, or outstanding rhetorical skill.

Leadership is a quality extraordinarily difficult to define. What is it that makes a man stand out in an assembly as an obvious leader, while others, richly endowed in other ways, pass by us unnoticed? Paul stands out in history as one of the great leaders –

pre-eminent among his contemporaries in this regard. Luke, the apostle's doctor-friend, has given us in the Acts a remarkable portrait of Paul in action, bold and unafraid,[6] alert in crisis,[7] shrewd in strategy.[8] And in the story of the great shipwreck, Luke shows that it was Paul, not the captain, who rallied the terrified crew, told the centurion and the soldiers what action should be taken, and had the common sense to urge those on board to have a good meal and take courage before eventually abandoning ship and making for the shore.[9]

It is very clear that there was nothing of the 'meek and mild' about this man. The Acts of the Apostles depicts a man who was something of a firebrand, certainly a character to be reckoned with, a man who naturally occupied the central place and elicited the attention of all in his company. We think of Paul's visit to Philippi. First, there was the happy scene of prayer and talk with the women and especially with Lydia, whose heart the Lord opened so that she responded to what Paul said. But that peaceful scene was followed by another of a very different character. We are introduced to the "slave-girl who was possessed by an oracular spirit", who followed Paul and kept shouting out day after day. Paul exorcised her; but the way Luke tells the story hints that the motive of his action was at least as much his desire for a bit of peace as compassion for the wretched girl – "Paul could bear it no longer. Rounding on the spirit he said, 'I command you . . . to come out of her.' "[10]

With even greater frankness, later in the same chapter the writer of the Acts shows us the apostle as a man who did not take insults and humiliation lying down. He and his friends had been flogged and imprisoned. The results were as painful to his dignity as they were to his body. News reached them through the converted jailer that the magistrates had sent instructions that they were to be released. The prisoner blazed with indignation. A public flogging of Roman citizens was not to be followed by a cowardly smuggling of them out in private. No indeed! "Let them come in person and escort us out."[11]

There was another stormy scene which Luke records with no attempt at hiding apostolic warts. The apostle stood before the chief priests and the entire Jewish Council. He began to address them, but was interrupted by the High Priest Ananias who ordered the attendants to strike Paul on the mouth. Did the apostle obey his Master's injunction to turn the other cheek? Not at all. He blazed out: "God will strike *you*, you whitewashed wall! You sit there to judge me in accordance with the Law; and then in defiance of the Law you order me to be struck!" True, an apology and something of a recantation followed the outburst; but the incident shows us a man with a temper, and a temper not always under control.[12]

The difference of opinion between Paul and Barnabas over John Mark is scarcely an instance of idyllic harmony. "The dispute was so sharp . . ." – the word used, if transliterated, is *paroxysm*. Paul could not forget that Mark had "deserted them in Pamphylia and had not gone on to share in their work". That dereliction of duty, as it seemed to him, still rankled, and it was left to the kindlier Barnabas to venture to give Mark another chance and take him with him on the work.[13]

The theme of *boasting* is a major one in the writings of Paul – and small wonder, for it was at that point precisely that the great change in his outlook, in his very religion, had taken place. (The verb to *boast, glory, pride oneself in*, occurs some thirty-five times in the Pauline literature.) Whereas, in his pre-conversion days, the source of his pride was in the Law and in his standing as a deeply committed Pharisee, now he boasted only in Christ and his cross. The change was radical. Any other kind of boasting, any place for human pride, was "excluded".[14] This was a recurrent emphasis in his thinking and in his writing.

But still from time to time in his letters he indulged in "the privilege of a fool", and had his "little boast like others". He was "not speaking as a Christian, but like a fool, if it comes to bragging".[15] The reference, it would seem, was half serious, half playful. He was proud of his independence – never would he sponge on the Corinthians, never be a burden to them. If this were regarded as pride on his part, he could not help it. Actually, it was because he loved them so much that he determined never to be a burden to them.[16]

In similar vein, he referred to his converts being a source of pride – "in Christ Jesus our Lord I am proud of you"; "I have great pride in you"; ". . . my pride in you has been justified".[17] This, surely, is justifiable pride; but the frequent recurrence of the idea and of the nouns and verb which convey it may well be indicative of how big a place pride took in his one-time experience and of how deep was the transformation which took place in him. His self-congratulation and self-boasting has changed – now he boasts in Christ Jesus, in his converts and, most surprising of all, in his present sufferings, that is to say, in what God had achieved by means of his weakness.[18]

Not without a struggle, however, did this once proud Pharisee live out a life of humility. Pride continued to rear its ugly head; the temptation was always there (is 2 Timothy 3: 10–11 an instance of his yielding to it? – ". . . my resolution, my faith, patience, and spirit of love, and my fortitude . . .").

An abrasive character? It would seem so. Certainly he was a man of great moral courage. If the truth as he saw it was at stake, if the purity of the Gospel was jeopardised, he was perfectly prepared to stand up and be counted. If need be, he would hurl an anathema at any who, out of weakness, went back on what they previously had acknowledged as new truth.[19]

The controversy with Peter, recorded with such heat in Galatians 2, provides us with an illustration of the depth of feeling which moved Paul when he saw someone abandoning a position which he knew to be right. The situation, in its main outline, is clear: Peter, conservative and bound by the old traditions which separated Jews from Gentiles, making (to take but one illustration) fellowship at table quite impossible, had finally come to the point where he saw that such one-time barriers were no longer relevant. In Christ the old divisions were no longer valid. Peter saw this – and it was a shattering revelation. He was true to it, and was prepared to abide by it *until* . . . "until certain persons came from James".[20] These were representatives, presumably, of a point of view which held that the old laws were still there to be obeyed, the old customs still to be followed. When these men came, Peter "drew back and began to hold aloof" (there is more than a suspicion, in the language used here, of a sting in the verbs which can be translated: "he turned his apostleship upside down and played the Pharisee").[21] Why did he do this? "Because he was afraid of the advocates of circumcision", the people who said that that old rite was incumbent on all who would enter the Christian Church. Paul saw that if they were followed, 'pillars' though they might be, Christianity, instead of being a faith open to the world, would be a mere sub-division of Judaism. This issue was quite crucial. On it, there could be no compromise. Paul might have anticipated the words of Martin Luther: "Here I stand. I can no other." The time had come to smite, not to caress.

The whole of the Epistle to the Galatians needs to be read, in order to feel the heat of the argument, the sternness towards the chief of the apostles, the deeply distressed but semi-humorous approach to the "dear idiots of Galatia", the rough, almost crude rebuke of the agitators, the pro-circumcision men, who "had better go the whole way and make eunuchs of themselves!"[22] This is Paul at his most polemical, the shepherd defending his sheep against the wolves, no matter what the cost might be to himself.

What we have said above represents only one side of a complex character. This man, strong, abrasive, judgmental, tempted to be proud, was a man who elicited the deepest devotion from his friends. In this very letter to the Galatians, the apostle points out that, when he had visited the people to whom he was writing, they showed no "scorn or disgust at the state of my poor body" – was he suffering from some unpleasant or infectious disease? They would have torn out their very eyes and given them to him, had that been possible – presumably the disease had affected his sight. They welcomed him as if he were an angel of God, as they might have received Christ Jesus himself![23] There must have been something deeply lovable in the man to elicit such self-sacrificing response. Indeed this is what we find, on Luke's testimony, in the Acts. There is a touching scene described in chapter 20. Paul had just completed his work, covering a considerable period of time, at Ephesus. He had called the elders of the church there to meet him at Miletus and had bidden them farewell. Now the time had come to say goodbye. Let the author of the Acts tell it in his own words – they call for no elaboration: "As he finished speaking, he knelt down with them all and prayed. Then there were loud cries of sorrow from them all, as they folded Paul in their arms and kissed him. What distressed them most was his saying that they would never see his face again. So they escorted him to his ship."[24]

A similar picture of deep affection for the apostle on the part of his friends is given us in the next chapter of the Acts. Paul had been staying for a week at Tyre with the disciples. They sensed danger for him when he told them of his prospective visit to Jerusalem. They urged him to abandon the project. The warning which the prophet Agabus gave that, if Paul went to Jerusalem, he would be bound and handed over to the Gentiles, only deepened the disciples' sense of foreboding. They "begged and implored Paul" to abandon his visit to Jerusalem. Their plea met with no response – Paul was convinced that the journey to Jerusalem was part of God's plan for him, and he could not be deterred. If it was to involve him in martyrdom, very well, so be it.[25]

But the language in which the story is told is indicative of the affection that Paul had drawn out of the people in his brief visit to Tyre.

The reason for this affection is not far to seek. It is abundantly clear that in the heart of this blunt, outspoken man there burned the passion of a pastor. Even in the stern letter to the Galatians we can detect an almost womanly tenderness. "Oh, my dear children," he writes, "I feel the pangs of childbirth all over again till Christ be formed within you, and how I long to be with you now! Perhaps I could then alter my tone to suit your mood. As it is, I honestly don't know how to deal with you."[26] He longs for them to "take the shape of Christ",[27] a phrase reminiscent of his statement in another letter, that God "ordained that we should be *shaped to the likeness of God's Son*".[28]

If, in this passage in Galatians, we see a womanly tenderness, in other epistles we see a fatherly care. The Corinthians, swollen-headed and wayward, had grieved not only God but also the apostle. He wrote to them "not . . . to shame you, but to bring you to reason; for you are my dear children. You may have ten thousand tutors in Christ, but you have only one father. For in Christ Jesus you are my offspring, and mine alone, through the preaching of the Gospel." So the 'mother' of the Epistle to the Galatians is the 'father' of the Corinthian correspondence. "Choose, then", he says, anticipating his visit to them with half a frown and half a smile, "am I to come to you with a rod in my hand, or in love and a gentle spirit?"[29] There is no doubt which of the two *he* would choose, given the chance!

Writing to the congregation of Thessalonians, Paul indulged in reminiscence. His ministry, when first he visited them, included a frank and fearless declaration of the Gospel, which scorned the use of flattery and abhorred any suggestion of greed. Though, as Christ's envoys, Paul and his companions, Silvanus and Timothy, might have made their weight felt, they preferred to be as gentle with the converts "as a nurse caring fondly for her children", or as a "father ... appealing to you by encouragement".[30]

The pictures of nurse and of father suggest a character full of love and sensitivity of approach. The apostle was fond of this father-child metaphor. It was more than a metaphor to him. In that most gentlemanly little note, the Epistle to Philemon, he pleaded with his owner for the slave Onesimus. He described the latter as "my child, whose father I have become in this prison". J. B. Phillips paraphrases the passage delightfully and, in doing so, brings out Paul's use of humour in getting his plea for leniency across to the slave-owner: "I am appealing to that love of yours, a simple personal appeal from Paul the old man, in prison for Jesus Christ's sake. I am appealing for my child. Yes, I have become a father though I have been under lock and key, and the child's name is – Onesimus!"[31] Who could refuse so winsome an appeal?

Another letter from prison gives us glimpses of a man who was deeply affectionate in his relationships with his friends. Whether the letter to the Philippians was written from Ephesus or from Rome matters little to our present purpose. The point is that it shows us a man to whom friendship and physical contact meant a very great deal. "God knows", he wrote, "how I long for you all, with the deep yearning of Christ Jesus himself."[32] So deep was his care for them that he found himself in something of a quandary: his expectation of "departing and being with Christ" filled him with such joyful anticipation that, in most ways, that would have been his first choice for the immediate future – and who could say whether the Roman authorities might not, at any moment, convert anticipation into reality? But there were other considerations to be borne in mind. He had a very special relationship with these dear friends in Philippi to whom he was writing. They had gone through a great deal together;[33] tribulation on behalf of the Gospel had forged a very close link between Paul and the members of the Philippian church. They needed him still. He was convinced that he would "stay, and stand by you all to help you forward and to add joy to your faith".[34] Heaven must wait for a while! There was work still to be done – at Philippi and at many another outpost of the Church.

Paul is an outstanding example of what the power of the Holy Spirit can do in the transformation of human character. How easily the very strength of the man's personality could have become brutality, the abrasiveness become bullying, the temptation to pride, if unresisted, an over-weening superiority! But this did not happen. The conversion experience set in motion within the man all the forces which changed the proud Pharisee into a humble and loving Christian. "My friends, beloved friends whom I long for, my joy, my crown, . . . my beloved!"[35] This was not emotionalism. This was the deep love of a man to whom friendship meant much and the strong bonds of friendship in Christ everything.

A passage such as the first half of Romans 16 can easily be skipped over lightly and regarded as little more than a string of names of people about whom we know very little. But it is much more than this. The way in which Paul describes them – the courtesy and care shown to Phoebe, the repeated "beloved" or "dear friend", the constant repetition of "together" which comes out more clearly in the Greek prefix *syn* than in the English translation, the delightful touch where he greets Rufus and, in greeting his mother, claims her as his own mother too (how many mothers had the apostle, scattered around the cities which he visited?) – all these things, little in themselves, mount up to show us a deeply affectionate character, and one to whom friendship was a vital component of life. "The kiss of peace" with which he bade his readers greet one another was no formality.[36] Sensitivity and courtesy and, indeed, a humility which is very remarkable in so forceful a personality, show themselves in many a passage in his letters. We can watch his growth, as the lordship of Christ became more and more dominant in his whole make-up. As the mind of Christ increasingly became his own, he grew in his liking of men, his understanding of men, his deep love of men. We are watching the growth of a soul.

Bornkamm can, without exaggeration, refer to "Paul's warmth of heart, his ability to identify himself to the full with others, his skill as a pastor, yes, and his sense of humour, which did not desert him even in prison."[37]

I have ventured to use the word 'humility' in describing the character of the apostle. Perhaps we might couple the word 'diffidence' with it. "To me, who am less than the least of all God's people, he has granted of his grace the privilege of proclaiming to the Gentiles the good news of the unfathomable riches of Christ . . ."[38] What can we infer from this reference to himself as "less than the least of all saints"? (The Greek word itself is unique in the New Testament.)[39] Is this a false humility – a kind of spiritual Uriah Heepishness – "see how humble I am"? I do not think so – and the reasons are many.

First, Paul could never forget that his hands had been stained with the blood of the Christians. He had "thoroughly approved" of Stephen's death.[40] That left an indelible mark on him – humbling him. *Secondly*, he was conscious of being in debt to Christ for everything that was good within him. That was not his achievement. It was Christ's achievement and he was the grateful recipient. *Thirdly*, in making this assertion to be "less than the least of God's people", he was simply putting himself in line with all those who have travelled far on the spiritual road. Let me mention but two: Xavier Schnieper, writing of Saint Francis of Assisi, said:

We know that Francis began by pursuing very worldly goals and it is also known that Francis never regarded himself as a saint but always described himself as a sinner. This was not due to any spiritual arrogance but to heartfelt honesty. He deliberately strove for the imitation of Christ, but to describe himself as a saint or to announce prophetically that he would one day be revered throughout the world as a saint would have been regarded by Francis of Assisi as a betrayal of Christ.[41]

Sigrid Undset, writing of Catherine of Siena, said:

> ... was Catherine really quite sincere when she sometimes called herself the worst of all sinners? Even Raimondo of Capua [her spiritual director, and biographer]had to confess that he had on occasion been doubtful. But in the end he learned to understand that Catherine measured perfection and imperfection with a yardstick which ordinary people do not know. Only God is perfect – this she had been allowed to see in her visions – and everything which is not God is imperfection.[42]

After all, Francis of Assisi and Catherine of Siena, and a host of others like them, were only sharing in the experience of Isaiah who, in the year that his hero-king Uzziah died in disgrace, "saw the Lord, high and lifted up" and, as a result, saw, as never before, not only the sin of his nation but also of himself. Not until he had been cleansed and seared by the flame from the altar could he dare to reply to the divine call, "Here am I: send me", and then only with the utmost diffidence could he go to fulfil it.[43] Moses hesitated;[44] Jeremiah held back;[45] Amos averred that he was not a prophet nor a prophet's son.[46] But to refuse the call would have been apostasy. These men could only go; and with a diffidence and a kind of awed surprise that to such as them should have come a divine summons and command.

"We have this treasure in earthen vessels." "We are no better than pots of earthenware to contain this treasure."[47] There was plenty of cause for humility and diffidence. There was every reason for Paul to face his task with "fear and trembling" not only when he went to Corinth, but also, we may be sure, on many another errand as well. Progressively he learnt that it was precisely when he was weak that he was strong.[48]

This hardly-come-by humility, this diffidence, this sensitivity, grew out of his suffering, physical and spiritual. It may be doubted whether there is any other soil – certainly there was no other soil so rich – out of which it could grow. Norman St John Stevas, interviewing the sculptress Elisabeth Frink on television in November 1981, asked her how she viewed Christ. She replied with two adjectives – "strong and vulnerable". Both words could be justified from all we know of the Master's character, this Man above all others whose strength, under perfect control, was manifested so often in gentleness and who was wounded in the house of his friends. But the description could also be applied to the apostle. Of his physical strength there can be little doubt – it is a matter for wonder that a man could survive the ordeals he sketched for us in one of his letters – "scourged, . . . imprisoned, many a time face to face with death. Five times the Jews have given me the thirty-nine strokes; three times I have been beaten with rods; once I was stoned; three times I have been shipwrecked, and for twenty-four hours I was adrift on the open sea. I have been constantly on the road; I have met dangers from rivers, dangers from robbers, dangers from my fellow-countrymen, dangers from foreigners, dangers in towns, dangers in the country, dangers at sea, dangers from false friends. I have toiled and drudged, I have often gone without sleep; hungry and thirsty, I have often gone fasting and I have suffered from cold and exposure."[49] He must have been physically very tough indeed. Of his strength of character we have already seen something in this chapter.

But "vulnerable"? Dante shrewdly says:

. . . as the thing's more perfect, more
it feels the good and so, likewise, the bane.[50]

73

If this is true, if it is a fact that "the mark of rank in Nature is capacity for pain", it would seem likely that Paul's 'vulnerability' increased as his spirituality progressed, vulnerability and sensitivity going together in a kind of holy alliance. A price has to be paid for the acquisition of the qualities of which we are speaking – and Paul paid it in ample measure.

Robin Daniels, after spending many hours of intimate talk with Yehudi Menuhin, the great violinist, wrote this perceptive paragraph about him: "All Menuhin's skill in violin playing, all his faculties of breadth of living and relating – I want these next words to be read as if underlined – have been hard-earned, and, at several fulcrum points in his life, were re-gained with difficulty, throb, and ache. The earlier the sun of genius rises, the darker the impending shadow may be."[51] We shall have more to say elsewhere about the thorn in the flesh to which Paul refers in 2 Corinthians 12: 7,[52] but we may remark here that surely that episode of "difficulty, throb and ache" was for him one of the "fulcrum points in his life", a point of extreme vulnerability, out of which his humility, his tenderness, his sensitivity sprang and steadily grew.

Let us summarise how far we have got in considering what Paul was really like. Something of a firebrand, at times abrasive, battling with the temptation to pride, holding very deep convictions, at times polemical, yet a man who elicited – and gave – deep affection and love, tender and fatherly, relying much on a host of friends, humble and diffident, sensitive and vulnerable. A big human being, some of whose marks of character seem to contradict other marks, he cannot neatly be summed up, as might lesser men.

Having said all this – and much more could be added – we have not yet really got to the heart of the man. Nor shall we do so unless and until we have looked carefully at a phrase which may well give us the key to the innermost chamber of the apostle's being. It is the phrase "in Christ".

74

Adolf Deissmann has reckoned that "the formula 'in Christ' (or 'in the Lord,' etc.) occurs 164 times in St Paul: it is really the characteristic expression of his Christianity."[53] At various eras of the Church's history, different aspects of Paul's teaching have been taken up, studied afresh, and applied with great power to the particular needs of the Church at those particular times. Now it is "justification by faith", the battle-cry of the Reformation. Now it is his teaching on sanctification; now, his emphasis on the Church; now, his exposition of the gifts of the Spirit, and so on. But if we want to understand the apostle, what it was that gave meaning to his life and became the prime source of his achievement, we must turn to the phrase "in Christ", and look it steadily in the face.

It is a strange phrase. We can scarcely find a parallel use to it in ordinary life. If, let us say, an intimate friend of Churchill who had spent many years with him and then had given a decade to the writing of his life were talking to us about that great man, he might sum up his relationship to him in a wide variety of ways. He might say that he feared him, or admired him, or revered him, or even loved him. But he never would say, "I am a man in Churchill." It would never occur to him to use such a phrase. But Paul was, above everything else, "a man in Christ".

Perhaps we can approach an understanding of the phrase best by use of analogies. We say of a fish that water is its element. In it, it lives, propagates, prospers. Out of it, even for a brief few moments, it dies. We say of a plant that earth is its element. Rooted securely in it, it lives and flourishes. Uprooted, it dies. We might say of the branch of a vine that the vine is its element. In it, it grows and produces fruit. Severed from it, it withers and dies. We say of the members of the animal world, including the members of the human race, that air is their element. It is literally our breath of life. Restrict our access to it, or submerge us in the alien element of water, and we die in a matter of seconds. We say of a man who is supremely happy in his vocation, fulfilled and absorbed in his work, reaching the fullness of his potential: "That man is in his element."

These analogies may help us, even if only partially, to understand what was in the mind of Paul when he spoke of a person being "in Christ". When a man is "in Christ", he is in his element, the element in which alone he can reach his fulfilment and come to the full stature of manhood, the destiny which God intended for him. This is no optional extra which a man, otherwise fully developed, might add for his enrichment, as he might adopt an interest in art or music or sport. For Paul to be out of Christ, to be cut off from Christ, would be to perish. Christ was the element in which he lived, in which he would die, in which he would rise again, the one, unchanging element which neither life could spoil nor death could take away. It was in the mind of the Creator that we "should be shaped to the likeness of his Son".[54] This is God's norm for humanity. To miss that is to live life in the shadows. Paul would go further, he would say that it is to die. He expressed the situation by means of a stark contrast: "Those who live on the level of our lower nature have their outlook formed by it, and that spells death; but those who live on the level of the spirit have the spiritual outlook, and that is life and peace."[55]

In his letters we can watch Paul struggling to put into words what "living on the spiritual level", being "in Christ", meant to him: "To me life is Christ, and death gain." J. B. Phillips' translation is something of a paraphrase, but it gets close to the sense of the verse: "Living to me means simply 'Christ', and if I die I should merely gain more of him."[56] Or again, in one of his earliest letters, the apostle wrote: "I have been crucified with Christ: the life I now live is not my life, but the life which Christ lives in me; and my present bodily life is lived by faith in the Son of God, who loved me and gave himself up for me."[57]

Clearly this was something which to Paul was very

intimate and deeply personal. He could not express it without the use of personal pronouns, and *singular* personal pronouns – "he loved me: he gave himself up for me".

But, in exploring the meaning of the phrase "in Christ", we cannot leave it at that. The personal pronouns are, and must be, singular, and we can thank God for that. But the concept of being "in Christ" is not exhausted when we think of it in terms of the singular. It is also, and essentially, a plural, a corporate, concept.

After his conversion on the Damascus road, Saul of Tarsus "was baptised".[58] Of what that particular incident in his spiritual pilgrimage meant to him, he tells us nothing. But that is not to say that he did not attach great importance to the sacrament. The reverse seems to have been the case. (When he thanked God that he "never baptised one of you – except Crispus and Gaius"[59] he was not minimising the importance of baptism. He was merely making the point that in this church at Corinth, where divisions were already all too apparent, no one could say that, having been baptised by Paul, he therefore belonged to the Paul party!) Baptism had for him the deepest significance. Let us look at two passages in the Epistle to the Romans which are baptismal, and which clearly indicate the communal nature of the sacraments and emphasise this 'community aspect' of being "in Christ".

The first passage is in the opening verses of Romans 6. Baptism is described as baptism "into union with Christ Jesus". It is also described as baptism "into his death". Just as Christ went down into death and rose in newness of life, so, when they were baptised, Christians went down into the water, died so far as the old life was concerned, and were raised to an altogether new plane of life. The language throughout the passage is plural. Baptism was a corporate experience as well as an individual one. A solitary Christian is a contradiction in terms. "All religious experience is ecclesiastical experience," as Bernard Lord Manning put it. Initiation into

Christ is initiation into his Body. To be "in Christ" is to be in his Body, with all that that entails of joy and sorrow, privilege and responsibility, jubilation and heart-break.

The second passage is in Romans 8, vv.15 ff. As the apostle wrote it, he may well have had in mind a scene the like of which was taking place in many parts of the Mediterranean world which he visited on his journeys. A little party of believers is wending its way towards the sea or towards a river, sometimes under cover of dark for security reasons. As the members of the party reach their destination, they take off their old garments. They go down to "burial" in the water and then come up again, alive with a new life, washed from their old sinful ways, the light of heaven in their eyes. Perhaps they put on a new white garment. Certainly they utter a great cry – how could they keep it in? "*Abba*! Father!" – the very word that Jesus had used with such awe and yet with such intimacy. "Abba! Father! We are in the family of which you are the head. We have a new relationship with you – we are your sons and daughters in the deepest sense. We are born into a family of brothers and sisters who, with us, have been baptised into union with Christ, who, like us, are in Christ. No more slavery! No more bondage! We are sons of God. We are brothers of one another. We all are in Christ."[60]

"If any man be in Christ, there is a new act of creation."[61] As in the old creation story in Genesis, God spoke and darkness gave way to light, chaos gave way to order, so it is in Christian experience. The Christian is "delivered from the domain of darkness and transferred . . . to the kingdom of his beloved Son",[62] the powers of death and of corruption having been overcome. Paul sought for illustrations by which to illuminate this all-embracing concept – and found them in plenty.

For example, he had much to say about "salvation". In fact, Anderson Scott makes this his dominant theme when he seeks to get to the heart of the apostle's life, thought and teaching. He calls it his "central and inclusive idea" . . . "the most comprehensive term for what the apostle found in Christ", embracing "all the great topics with which we are familiar – Redemption, Justification, Reconciliation, Adoption, Sanctification."[63]

All Paul's Jewish readers would have been familiar with the concept of "salvation" as having a *military* nuance, for the Old Testament was full of references to the salvation which Yahweh wrought when he rescued his people from the power of their enemies. Indeed, the very word is that which we find in the proper name Joshua, which in its Greek form is Jesus.

Or again, when Paul spoke of justification – "justified by faith, we have peace with God"[64] – he was using a *judicial* metaphor to indicate the new status which the child of God has in Christ. He has been acquitted. He has been put right.

The concept of being "in Christ" is so central to Paul's experience and teaching, and is so vital for an understanding of the meaning of the Christian faith, that it will be worthwhile to pause at this point in order to note how close to this concept does another great writer of the New Testament come. I refer to the author of the Fourth Gospel, and especially to his teaching about the Vine and the branches.[65] It is clear that in the opening verses of John 15, the claim is being made that Jesus and his disciples, in a wonderful unity, are the real, genuine Israel of God – the new society of Jesus has superseded the ancient theocracy. This is the point of the adjective 'real' – the 'real' vine. The Old Testament Church had failed the Lord who had planted and tended it with such care.[66] Looking back, that Church can now be seen as a sad travesty of what was in the mind of God. The true, eternal, spiritual reality has now arrived in Christ and his disciples.

It is noteworthy that John does not say that Christ is the root or stem. He says that he is the vine itself. Vine and branches are one organic unity. Paul does much the same thing when he stresses the unity of Christ and the

Church under the picture of the head and the limbs together making up one Body. "Just as the body is one and has many members, and all the members of the body, though many, are one body, so it is with" – with what? The Church – that is what we would have expected him to write. But no. "So it is with *Christ*".[67] "He calls the Church Christ," Calvin comments. "Christ and Christians are *quasi una persona mystica*," says St Thomas Aquinas. John and Paul are at one.

Mrs H. E. Hamilton King, in her too-little-known poem *The Disciples*,[68] captures the thought of John and his picture of the Vine. But she could equally well have been expounding Paul and his picture of the Body:

The Living Vine, Christ chose it for Himself:–
God gave to man for use and sustenance
Corn, wine, and oil, and each of these is good
And Christ is Bread of Life, and Light of Life.
But yet He did not choose the summer corn,
That shoots up straight and free, in one quick growth,
And has its day, and is done, and springs no more;
Nor yet the olive, all whose boughs are spread
In the soft air, and never lose a leaf,
Flowering and fruitful in perpetual peace:
But only this for Him and His in one, –
The everlasting, ever quickening Vine,
That gives the heat and passion of the world,
Through its own life-blood, still renewed and shed.

It was Paul's supreme glory to realise that he was "a man in Christ". God had made him for this. He was the heir of a faith which held that man is made "in the image of God". True, that image had been defaced, in him and in all his fellow human-beings, for "all have sinned, and all fall short of God's splendour".[69] But the basic fact remained, man "*is* made in the image of God", is indeed "little lower than the angels".[70] Paul can be regarded as the great humanist. He may have known –

he certainly could have made his own – the words of the Roman comic dramatist, Terence (c.190–159 BC): *Homo sum. Humani nihil a me alienum puto* – "I am a man. I count nothing human indifferent to me."[71] For Paul, that manhood was seen in its fullest light, in its truest colours, when it was grasped that, for man's redemption, the Son of God "was contented to be betrayed, and given up into the hands of wicked men, and to suffer death upon the cross".[72] "My worth is what I am worth to God; and that is a marvellous great deal, for Christ died for me."[73] To be "in Christ" is to realise one's manhood as God intended it to be.

It is no wonder that Paul's theology often found its climax in doxology. Pondering the ways of God in history, he wrote: "O depth of wealth, wisdom, and knowledge in God! How unsearchable his judgements, how untraceable his ways! . . . Source, Guide, and Goal of all that is – to him be glory for ever! Amen."[74] Writing of God's way with his Church, he ended another passage: "Now to him who is able to do immeasurably more than all we can ask or conceive, by the power which is at work among us, to him be glory in the church and in Christ Jesus from generation to generation evermore! Amen."[75] Thinking of Christ's sacrifice for his sins, to rescue him "out of this present age of wickedness, as our God and Father willed", he found himself compelled to slip in his tribute of praise – "to whom be glory for ever and ever. Amen."[76]

The note of doxology can never be far from the lips of a man "redeemed, restored, forgiven", a man "in Christ". Charles Raven, theologian and scientist, wrote of his Lord: "He takes us, and fills us with a life not our own, a life which is beyond sorrow and romance: he takes us, and in his grip we live abundantly, sharing for a moment the activity of his overwhelming love."[77]

F. W. H. Myers, in his poem *St Paul*, gets close to the heart of Christian experience:

Who that one moment has at least descried him,
Dimly and faintly, hidden and afar,
Does not despise all excellence beside him,
Pleasures and powers that are not and that are?

This hath he done and shall we not adore him?
This shall he do and can we still despair?
Come let us quickly fling ourselves before him,
Cast at our feet the burthen of our care.

Flash from our eyes the glow of our thanksgiving,
Glad and regretful, confident and calm,
Then thro' all life and what is after living
Thrill to the tireless music of a psalm.

Yea, thro' life, death, thro' sorrow and thro' sinning,
He shall suffice me, for he hath sufficed.
Christ is the end, for Christ is the beginning,
Christ the beginning, for the end is Christ.

George Herbert, seventeenth-century poet and divine, puts it quaintly, in his own gentle way, but none the
less forcefully for that, in his poem *Aaron*:

> Christ is my only head,
> My alone only heart and breast,
> My only music, striking me ev'n dead;
> That to the old man I may rest,
> And be in Him now drest.[78]

Paul. His name in Latin means small. In fact, he was
a man made on a massive scale, one of the few men of
ancient history who can truly be called great, a man
re-made, a man "in Christ".

GROWTH

Man dwells at that point of the universe, poised between the pull of the earthly and the heavenly, where God can cross over and reach him and render unto him grace.

Simone Weil: *Gravity and Grace*

God's love to us is shown in his respect for our own individuality. God loves us so much that he does not withhold suffering from us.

Martin Israel: *The Spirit of Counsel*

Put love first; but there are other gifts of the Spirit at which you should aim also . . .

1 Corinthians 14: 1

Aim at peace with all men, and a holy life, for without that no one will see the Lord.

Hebrews 12: 14

5

GROWTH

To trace the growth of a soul is to engage on a task of great delicacy. When that soul is one of the greatest figures in the life of the Church, as Paul undoubtedly was, even greater delicacy and insight are called for. And when the correspondence left by the person concerned is relatively small and, further, covers only a fairly short period of his life, the task has added difficulty. The editor of the correspondence of John Henry Newman, for example, has at his disposal a huge mass of material, as those who have handled the thirty-five volumes of Father C. S. Dessain's monumental work can see. It is likely that no great difficulty will be found in tracing the growth of the writer revealed in those hundreds of letters. The man who handles the correspondence of Paul, on the other hand, has infinitely less to go on, and therefore must tread the more warily if he is seeking to discern the work of the Spirit on the man's sensitive personality – growth here, change there, less stress on a subject here, more emphasis on the same subject there. Caution is called for.

None the less, it is, I believe, possible to trace changes of emphasis, to detect evidence of growth, to watch spiritual deepening, to distinguish intellectual development. It will be the purpose of this chapter to seek to do this. If we succeed, we shall be watching the way of God with a man of his choosing – and that is always a ploy worth pursuing.

First, we may touch upon a couple of instances where we *may* – I emphasise 'may' – detect a change of emphasis as the earlier letters give way to the later. The first has to do with Paul's attitude to the Jews, the second with his attitude to the coming advent of Christ.

The Thessalonian correspondence (together with the Epistle to the Galatians) is generally agreed to be the earliest that we have from Paul's pen. The first letter contains this passage: "You have been treated by your countrymen as they are treated by the Jews, who killed the Lord Jesus and the prophets and drove us out, the Jews who are heedless of God's will and enemies of their fellow-men, hindering us from speaking to the Gentiles to lead them to salvation. All this time they have been making up the full measure of their guilt, and now retribution has overtaken them for good and all."[1]

These are tough words. We might be forgiven if we saw in them an almost bitter reaction on the part of the apostle to the reception accorded to him by his fellow-Jews when he presented the Gospel to them and they refused it. Had he known the appalling story which history was to record of 'Christian' relationships with the Jews, had he been able to foresee the atrocities of the Crusaders, not to mention the unspeakable holocaust of the Nazi regime, had he been able to read the work of Marcion and – far worse – that of Martin Luther in his later years, had he been able to sense the revulsion of a sensitive Jew when his people are referred to as "God-killers", his language might have been more gentle.

The attitude of the real Paul towards the Jews is, surely, better reflected in such a passage as this: "In my heart there is great grief and unceasing sorrow. For I could even pray to be outcast from Christ myself for the sake of my brothers, my natural kinsfolk. They are Israelites: they were made God's sons; theirs is the splendour of the divine presence, theirs the covenants, the law, the temple worship, and the promises. Theirs are the patriarchs, and from them, in natural descent, sprang the Messiah." Or again: "Brothers, my deepest desire and my prayer to God is for their salvation . . . " And again: "I ask, then, has God rejected his people? I cannot believe it! I am an Israelite myself, of the stock of

Abraham, of the tribe of Benjamin. No! God has not rejected the people which he acknowledged of old as his own."[2] The Epistle to the Romans is later than the Thessalonian correspondence. Can we trace here a development in his approach?

In his attitude to the second advent of Christ, we may detect another instance of adjustment. It is clear that in the early days of his writing ministry, he viewed that advent as imminent. There were Christians in Thessalonica who were puzzled as to what they should believe about fellow-Christians who had died without having seen Christ in his re-appearance on earth. He wrote to assure them that God had a plan for them as well as for those still alive on earth. But Paul clearly was thinking in terms of many of his contemporaries, probably including himself, being present when the Lord came – "we who are left alive until the Lord comes" obviously indicates such a belief.[3]

As the years passed by and the final intervention of God in history had not taken place, Paul did not abandon the doctrine, but, when he wrote of the matter, he seems to have put less emphasis on its immediacy.[4]

Turning now to the man himself, we can trace a deepening in the spiritual life of the apostle. This, it seems clear, is closely connected with his experience of *suffering* – in several spheres.

At the heart of one of the most intimate autobiographical passages in Paul's writings, he asserts that, for the sake of Christ, he "*suffered the loss of all things*" and counted them "but dung".[5] To "suffer the loss of all things" is a phrase which catches the imagination and makes one wonder. What were these "all things"? He speaks of things which, in his pre-Christian period, were "gain to him". We can well imagine these – the pride of his parents as they watched the boy, the adolescent, the young man maturing in the way of Jewish orthodoxy. This meant much to him. Who could tell – he might be another Gamaliel, or a greater than Gamaliel! Perhaps the boy himself nursed some such ambition.

Then came the break. Was there a painful scene at the parting of the ways, when his parents could not stomach the new doctrines which their son was espousing? Did "the loss of all things" include their refusal to welcome him to the parental home, a severance from the domestic and financial inheritance which otherwise would have been his?

Then there was the highly civilised life of Tarsus and Jerusalem, the culture of the universities, the companionship of scholarly minds, the world of books and ideas, the study of the law and, no doubt, side-glances at the philosophies of Stoics and others. These things were very dear to this town-centred man with the scintillating, out-reaching mind. As, on his missionary journeys, he tramped the weary miles, or rode his donkey, or sailed on perilous seas, his mind must often have turned back to the easier life of the scholar which he had loved and, later, abandoned for Christ's sake.

I thought of him often as I recently covered some of the ground which he travelled in Turkey. True, the car which carried me seemed to have some of its parts held together with pieces of string, but we covered our distances with speed and with a measure of comfort. Paul travelled perhaps fifteen miles a day, "in weariness and painfulness". On my journey, I was impressed by the sheer beauty of the landscape. It was spring-time and the land was burgeoning with life. The peach trees were beginning to blossom – there was a haze of deep pink set off against a background of dark soil. The trees were budding – a filigree-work of yellowish-green as tender as the winter they had endured was long and hard. It was a land of apples, figs, grapes and nuts in rich abundance. The land which had silted up and strangled Ephesus and Miletus as ports was now a great alluvial plain, rich in crops, producing cotton in plenty. The variety of colour in the soils was enough to delight the heart of any artist, melting, sometimes, into a deep pink which seemed to reflect the complexion of some of the people themselves, whose dark skin looked as if a kindly

88

brush had touched its surface with red. There were sheep and goats in plenty in Cilicia, constant reminders that it was with good reason that it had given its name to *cilicium*, the goat's hair which Paul, himself a tent-maker, had often used in his work.[6]

Yet, for all the beauty and the plenty, there was a ferocity about the land where Paul undertook some of his most effective journeys. The Taurus mountains are riven, scarred by fierce heat and bitter cold. The land is battered, weather-beaten by the storms of long millennia. It can be no fun to be exposed to the ferocity of such weather. As Paul turned his back on the comforts of his one-time home, it must have called for superb endurance to expose himself to the furies of nature as he tramped from Tarsus to Iconium, to Hierapolis, to Ephesus, to Miletus . . . "I have been constantly on the road; I have met dangers from rivers, dangers from robbers, . . . dangers in the country, dangers at sea . . . I have toiled and drudged, I have often gone without sleep; hungry and thirsty, I have often gone fasting; and I have suffered from cold and exposure."[7] "I have suffered the loss of all things . . ." "Endure hardness as a good soldier of Jesus Christ"[8] – this was a stark reality to the man of the city who tramped the country, weary mile after weary mile.

Then there was that "thorn in the flesh" of which Paul spoke so movingly.[9] What was it? Martin Luther wrote: "Paul's 'thorn in the flesh' means *fidei tentatio*, the tempting of our faith. He saw it as a big skewer to impale our soul and our flesh. It was not sexual temptation as the papists suppose – knowing no other temptations than sexual ones and never having experienced great wrestlings of faith."[10] It may be doubted whether he was right in so 'spiritualising' that which attacked Paul. The thorn in the flesh may well have *resulted* in a tempting of his faith, though it is doubtful whether it can be compared with Luther's despair of God's grace. It was, much more probably, something severely physical. Luther's "big skewer" is close to the meaning of the

Greek word which Paul uses. Its very sound, *skolops*, is menacing! It can be used of a fish-hook, or a sharp stake such as is used in palisades. It is something which, entering the flesh, makes it bleed. Was it a recurring splitting headache, which seemed like a stake driven into his temples, inducing a depression which was the obverse side of the coin of his spiritual exaltation? Was it malaria, easily caught in the swampy lands through which he travelled? We do not know. What is clear is that it was something which humiliated him, like the disease he obliquely refers to in another letter – "you showed neither scorn nor disgust at the trial my poor body was enduring".[11] It held up the work which he longed to pursue with undiminished energy. It seemed to be a messenger sent straight from Satan to bruise him.

What was he to do when this seeming disaster hit him? He did what any sensible disciple of Jesus would do – he prayed, not once, nor twice, but thrice. "I begged the Lord to rid me of it." Perhaps it would have been better if he had simply prayed, "thy will be done", as the Lord had done in Gethsemane. But his prayer was a natural one, and received an answer. The answer was a firm 'No'. A father often has to give such an answer to a child's request, because the father can see how disastrous an affirmative answer would be. The child is perplexed, but the father knows. Later on, the child understands.

For Paul that negative answer led to something which might almost be called a second conversion – such an experience of God as revolutionised him. No longer would he fight this stake in the flesh. If God was not going to remove it, it presumably had within it the makings of a blessing. In the heart of the trial was to be found a revelation of the grace of God. "My grace is all you need; power comes to its full strength in weakness." So he was "well content with weakness, contempt, persecution, hardship and frustration". Over him, like a shade from the blazing sun, the power of Christ came.

All was well. John Hutton writes of a man allowing "his private grief or anxiety, even his private shame . . . to take him deeply towards God, to take him down and down until he is alone, and yet not alone".[12] That is what Paul did with his *skolops*. A new way was opened up to the living God and his life-giving Spirit. It was not the way of evasion – not "out of" but "in"; not "around" but "through". "*In the midst* of the fire" was found one "like a son of the gods".[13] "When thou passest *through* the waters, I will be with thee".[14] Put in another way, we can say that God had a way with the apostle of turning what he regarded as a minus into a plus, a tragic minor into a triumphant major chord.

It is not simply that, in the mystery of things, suffering seems to be a necessary constituent of life – "take away sharps and flats, and there is no music; take away suffering, and there is no life".[15] The Christian sees his God as engaged in the suffering. Without that insight, suffering can easily lead to bitterness; with it, to sweetness and victory. Paul speaks of a "wound which is borne in God's way" and which "brings a change of heart too salutary to regret", while "the hurt which is borne in the world's way brings death".[16] It is a salutary insight. That sensitive writer, Elizabeth Goudge, suggests that it is

how an individual takes his pain, what he allows it to do in him and through him [that] is much more important than the pain itself. The scene of suffering in each person seems to be a battleground where a thing evil in its origin comes up against the battling love of God that would transform it into an instrument of victory; not victory for the individual alone but also for God himself in the cosmic battle between good and evil.[17]

Dr Frank Lake writes:

It is much more than forgiveness that Christ's death offers us . . . The opening verses [of 2 Corinthians 1] speak of affliction, which crushes the spirit to death and worse if it has to be borne alone, unless the divine-human comfort of God, acting through those who have been comforted in their affliction, turns it to shared suffering. This transformation of destructive affliction into creative suffering is, for St Paul, a vital mode of Christ's action and passion. The glory of God is revealed in the face of Jesus Christ . . . not just because he forgives sins, but because he is totally with us in our affliction.[18]

This Christians believe. This has been proved true, tested out by the saints again and again. But very often suffering – physical, mental, nervous – is of such a sort that all *sense* of the presence of God in its midst is denied to the sufferer. In fact, the acutest part of the suffering is precisely this, that the sufferer has no realisation of the presence of the Lord with him, at that point. All is blackness and darkness. What then? We can call to mind that this seems to have been exactly what happened to our Lord himself, when "horror and dismay" came over him in the garden of Gethsemane, and when, at his trial, he was reduced to silence by his sufferings – he had nothing to say. At those terrible moments he encapsulated in himself the bitterest of human agony.

For Maxsymilian Kolbe, the Polish martyr who gave his life at Auschwitz so that the father of a family might go free, suffering was "the fire that purifies everything" – "all these trials are useful, necessary, and even indispensable, like the crucible where gold is purified".[19] The torture camp was "the crucible of affliction to fire Christian love".[20]

John Milton, afflicted with blindness, could not regard it as the ultimate disaster. He wrote: "To be sure, we blind men are not the least of God's concerns, for the less able we are to perceive anything other than Himself, the more mercifully and graciously does He deign

to look upon us."[21] The man who could write, in his
Paradise Regained,

> Who best
> Can suffer, best can do; best reign, who first
> Well hath obeyed

knew, albeit in a more 'stoical' and less profoundly
Christian way than Paul, how to find in the heart of
suffering something very positive.

There was, then, for Paul the suffering of "the loss of
all things", and there was physical suffering with its
consequent mental and nervous effects. But there was
more – and here, it may well be, the hurt went deepest.
Paul was a sensitive soul. Treachery, disloyalty on the
part of his friends, cut right into him. Scattered through
his writings there are allusions to such things, all the
more poignant for their brevity, unelaborated because
it pained him to dwell on them. "Dangers from false
friends" – the phrase is tucked away in the long list of
trials that he gives us.[22] There was the obstinacy of the
Jewish brethren to whom he went first on his entry into
the towns he was evangelising – the ground was hard,
and he turned to the Gentiles with an ache in his heart.
There was the incident of John Mark whom Paul judged
to have "deserted them in Pamphylia and" [who] "had
not gone on to share in their work".[23] There was Demas
who "has deserted me because his heart was set on this
world"[24] – what lay behind that accusation, we may
wonder? Not everyone was prepared to "suffer the loss
of all things"!

Again, there were those severe letters he had to write,
such as that to the Corinthians which, if it hurt them to
receive, hurt him much more to write. "That letter I
sent you came out of great distress and anxiety; how
many tears I shed as I wrote it! But I never meant to
cause you pain; I wanted you rather to know the love,
the more than ordinary love, that I have for you."[25] And
those Galatians – "O you dear idiots of Galatia, who

saw Jesus Christ the crucified so plainly, who has been casting a spell over you?"[26] How can they be so stupid as to slip back when once they have seen the splendour of the Christian way?

Suffering can be – often is – a source of bitterness in the development of character. It can be a point of growth. For Paul it was a basic element of that spiritual deepening which we are considering in this chapter. So far from separating him from God, it drove him closer to him.

Neville Cardus, musical critic and lover of cricket, described himself as an agnostic, but he wrote understandingly when, like the rest of us, he found himself wrestling with the problem of suffering.

> Supposing, by a great stretch of imagination, I picture myself as the Creator. I would not make the world a completely happy place. I would allow disasters and tragedies to happen; otherwise people wouldn't acquire a sense of the mystery of life, and we would have none of the great masterpieces of art. We would feel only half alive if we had no trials, no tests. As Creator, I'd make it very difficult for mortal beings to believe in me. I wouldn't want anyone to say, 'Thank you, God: I believe in you because I am happy.' I would want people to say: 'I believe in you because you've been cruel as well as kind to me. You've tested me. Why have you done this? There must be a reason. You must value me or you wouldn't take the trouble to send occasional tragedy into my life.'[27]

Paul would have understood what Cardus was getting at, however fumblingly. But he would have gone – indeed, he went – much further because he believed in a God who had disclosed himself in Christ. Not that all of his problems had been thereby solved – far from it. But at least he caught glimpses, and things began to piece together, to make sense, *viewed in the light of eternity*. There is much about suffering in the opening chapters of his second letter to the Corinthians. But for sheer spiritual insight Paul reaches the climax of his argument when he writes: "Though our outward humanity is in decay, yet day by day we are inwardly renewed. Our troubles are slight and short-lived; and their outcome an eternal glory which outweighs them far. Meanwhile our eyes are fixed, not on the things that are seen, but on the things that are unseen. For what is seen passes away; what is unseen is eternal."[28] There is a perspective here which is open only to the man of faith.

To such a perspective Paul returns in a classic passage. He begins: "I reckon that the sufferings we now endure bear no comparison with the splendour, as yet unrevealed, which is in store for us." Suffering cannot embitter a man upheld by such a hope and sustained with such a prospect. Of this we shall have more to say in a later chapter.[29]

There was another area of growth and development, in a sense separate from but allied to Paul's personal spiritual growth. It was a development in his concept of his missionary task and, beyond that, the missionary task of the Church. To this we must now turn.

As we have seen, there are three accounts of the conversion of Paul in the Acts.[30] Whatever precisely happened on the Damascus road, it would seem clear that, at the time of his conversion or shortly after, a sense of mission beyond the bounds of his own people came home to him. But the significance and implications of that call, glimpsed when the light from heaven shone on him, needed working out. A seed had been sown. It would take time to grow into a tree.

We have suggested that Paul's stay in Arabia gave him the opportunity to begin to think out this larger strategy.[31] He would have done so against the background of his Hebrew Scriptures which now took on a deeper meaning than he had ever seen in them before. For example, in the Servant Songs of Second Isaiah the mission of Israel is depicted in terms which reach out far beyond the bounds of Israel itself. Her mission is to be understood not in terms of privilege but of responsibility to spread the light which has been given her in trust. Thus: "I, the Lord, have called you with righteous purpose and taken you by the hand; I have formed you and appointed you to be a light *to all peoples*, a beacon for *the nations*, to open eyes that are blind, to bring captives out of prison, out of the dungeons where they lie in darkness."[32] And again: "It is too slight a task for you, as my servant, to restore the tribes of Jacob, to bring back the descendants of Israel: I will make you a light to *the nations*, to be my salvation to *earth's farthest bounds*."[33] The writer of the last chapter of Isaiah goes so far as to envisage the day when God would take some "from every nation" to be even priests and Levites.[34] And Isaiah was not alone in being an instrument of this larger vision.[35]

All this tied in with the vision that had come to Paul – could it be that, in the purpose of God, he was to be an instrument in bringing to fruition the vision which the prophets had glimpsed, and doing so with a content which only Christ had been able to give to it? Arabia helped in the process of clarifying Paul's mind. Perhaps some successes which God gave him in his evangelistic work there helped to confirm his call and his interpretation of it as a part-fulfilment of the prophets' vision. But it is likely that it was only when he was well launched on his missionary journeys that the full significance dawned on him and the full strategy opened up. In his letter to the Galatians, he only mentions the thirteen or fourteen years which he spent in "the regions of Syria and Cilicia", but A. D. Nock is doubtless right in saying that they "must have been of supreme importance in Paul's evolution, for during them he was engaged in missionary activity to the Gentiles and he had need and time to develop his personal theology and his technique of preaching and argument".[36]

A critical point in the development of his missionary strategy would seem to have been reached when, the

Holy Spirit having prevented him and his companions from going south-west into the Roman Province of Asia Minor, and having forbidden them to go northward to Bithynia, they went to Troas where, in a dream, Paul received the divine direction to go into Macedonia.[37] There Philippi, the Roman outpost at the beginning of the Egnatian Way, was the point whence all eyes looked to Rome. Much was to happen to him before he reached that centre of the world – much missionary work, a journey to Jerusalem to carry the offerings of the Christian churches, and so on. But the strategy was clear: Rome – "I must see Rome";[38] and beyond Rome, Spain. The world for Christ! Such was the growth, the development, of his missionary vision. It was strategy on the big scale.

As he worked things out, tramping the long miles or waiting weary months for a ship when the Mediterranean was all but closed during the winter, he must have seen how marvellous had been his own preparation for the part that he was to play in God's strategy. Tarsus, the proud city of his birth, has been called "the buckle which bound East to West. There is a certain inevitability in the fact that the man who was chosen to interpret Christianity to the West should have come from that city which, above all others in the Hellenistic world, was a perfect amalgamation of Orient and Occident."[39] With his understanding of "the tension between the ghetto and the gym" (to use a phrase of Stuart Blanch's which admirably sums up what it meant to grow up as a Jew in Tarsus), Paul was perfectly suited to be the architect of the mission which saw Christ as the universal Lord, whose meaning and message were meant for, *and must reach*, all men under the sun.

So far, in this chapter, we have traced something of the spiritual growth of Paul, often, perhaps primarily, through suffering. We have traced, too, something of the growth of his concept of his missionary task. There was nothing static about this man – spiritual and intellectual development went hand in hand. In later chapters[40] we shall see how his growing and fertile mind reached out, beyond the death of the body and beyond the confines of this little world, to the End, the great consummation in the mind of God. In this chapter, and in those, we see the apostle as a man who, in his own person, illustrates Anselm's definition of religion as *fides quaerens intellectum*, faith seeking understanding. It was a noble quest, nobly pursued.

THINKER AND WRITER

... the worship offered by mind and heart ... Let your
minds be remade and your whole nature thus transformed.

Romans 12: 1 and 2

Those in whom the intellect has taken precedence over
the spiritual, the heart, they are the ones who are
gullible, who fall for the temptation of the clever wiles
of Marxism.

Alexander Solzhenitsyn in conversation
with Bernard Levin
(*The Times*, 23 May, 1983)

He cannot be comprehended by our intellect or any
man's – or any angel's for that matter. For both we and
they are created beings. But only to our intellect is he
incomprehensible: not to our love.

The Cloud of Unknowing, tr. C. Wolters

He may well be loved, but not thought. By love he can be
caught and held, but by thinking never.

ibid.

Newman was an intellectual who distrusted the intellect.

Owen Chadwick: *Newman*

6

THINKER AND WRITER

"Canst thou by searching find out God?"[1] Job's friend Zophar the Naamathite left us in no doubt that his answer to the question was an unqualified 'No'.

If we put the question in the form of the New English Bible translation – "Can you fathom the mystery of God, can you fathom the perfection of the Almighty?" – the answer is again 'No'. There is an abyss of mystery about deity before which man can only stand in the silence begotten of awe and of a sense of his own littleness. Zophar's reply to this question was: "It is higher than heaven; you can do nothing. It is deeper than Sheol; you can know nothing." With that answer, Paul would at least have had a deep sympathy.

There is a certain nervousness about the way in which he speaks of man's knowledge. "Of course," he says, quoting his Corinthian correspondents, "we all 'have knowledge'." But immediately he warns: "This 'knowledge' breeds conceit . . . If anyone fancies that he knows, he knows nothing yet, in the true sense of knowing."[2] "I may have all knowledge . . . but if I have no love, I am nothing." Knowledge "will vanish away".[3]

That nervousness in speaking about knowledge may have derived in part from Paul's encounter with certain forms of thought of a Gnostic flavour which implied that knowledge was the way through to Reality. The way to God, the ascent from human material existence to the infinite, was by means of a series of steps on the ladder of knowledge. Paul would have none of this. His own experience contradicted it. In his pre-conversion days, he had knowledge in abundance – was he not a pupil of Gamaliel? Had he not sat at the feet of the best teachers that Judaism could provide? Did he not come from a family whose chief joy was found in the knowledge of the law? All very true. But it was only in a moment of *revelation* that he entered into life as he now knew it as a Christian. He did not receive the Gospel "from any man; no man taught it me; I received it through a revelation of Jesus Christ."[4] "The world failed to find God by its wisdom."[5] Such wisdom always has about it the marks of the ephemeral, even of folly in the eyes of God.[6] But "the light of *revelation* – the revelation of the glory of God in the face of Jesus Christ"[7] – is of an entirely different genre. *This* is the result of the initiative of divine love. Paul knew what he was speaking about. The Hound of Heaven had sought him and found him, had known him long before the future apostle sought him. The divine love had invaded him – breached the barriers. Now he could rejoice in the pre-venient knowledge and grace of God. Now he could respond in the obedience of faith, his one consuming passion being summed up in the longing to know the unknowable love of God.

Perhaps his finest expression of this passion is found in the spiritual-autobiographical passage in the letter to the Philippians – "I count everything sheer loss . . . I count it so much garbage, for the sake of gaining Christ and finding myself incorporate in him . . . All I care for is to know Christ, to experience the power of his resurrection, and to share his sufferings . . ."[8]

When a man has been laid hold of by God and when he begins to see the glory of God in the face of Jesus Christ, he enters a sphere in which experiential knowledge comes into its own. This is no mere intellectual assent or achievement. This is "insight into the will" of God which results in a manner of life worthy of and entirely pleasing to the Lord.[9] This negates at once any possibility of a knowledge which is airy-fairy and unrelated to life. This roots it firmly in the soil of everyday living and discipleship. This is the knowledge of the Son of God which is the mark of "mature manhood".[10]

Learning alone, knowledge by itself, had not availed to bring Paul into the relationship with God which he now enjoyed in Christ. Knowledge and the wisdom that is from above were two very different things. The saints have perceived this. Thomas à Kempis wrote: "All men naturally desire knowledge; but what profit is there in knowledge without the fear of God? Certainly, a lowly peasant who serves God is better than a proud philosopher, who, to the neglect of his own soul, studies the course of the heavens."[11] St Francis of Assisi got to the heart of the matter when he prayed: "Give me, O Lord, wisdom and discernment to understand thy true and holy will." The poets and musicians understand this better than do most. T. S. Eliot posed the question: "Where is the wisdom we have left in knowledge?" And Yehudi Menuhin, writing in praise of Neville Cardus, went far to answer Eliot's question: "We are inclined to assume that 'understanding' itself implies analysis and, finally, a sum of parts, but true understanding must always mean much more, for sympathy and love exceed the analytical, just as, conversely, prejudice and hate defy reason. Neville Cardus reminds us that there is an understanding of the heart as well as of the mind."[12]

If, however, we were to leave the matter here, it might be thought that we were saying that, after and as a result of his conversion experience, Paul turned his back on the intellectual side of human existence and abandoned an intelligent approach to life, its problems and its challenges. Nothing could be further from the truth. Indeed we shall only understand Paul when we regard him as the apostle, indeed the champion, of the dedicated mind.

'Repentance' (*metanoia*) in the New Testament is essentially a change of *mind*. The man who repents is a man who thinks things through – his attitude to God, to his neighbour, to himself, to reality – in such a way that his whole outlook is changed; a revolution takes place. He turns his back on the old way of looking at things. He faces right about, his thinking and hence his acting wholly changed. The word (repentance) and its verb (to repent) are of frequent occurrence in the Gospels, in the Acts, and in the Revelation. In the Pauline writings they are comparatively rare. But that is not to say that the concept was unimportant to Paul. Not so. "Do you think lightly", he asks his Roman readers, "of [God's] wealth of kindness, of tolerance, and of patience, without recognising that God's kindness is meant to lead you to *a change of heart*?"[13] – the word is repentance, change of mind and action. God, the apostle is saying, delayed his judgement, and extended his compassion, in order to give you a chance to *think again* and change your ways. Writing to the Corinthians about a wound which had caused his readers suffering, he points out that a wound "borne in God's way brings *a change of heart* too salutary to regret; but the hurt which is borne in the world's way brings death."[14] It all depends on how you react when you put this wound into your thinking process and face it intelligently. Again, at the end of that same letter, Paul writes of his fear of finding, on his arrival at Corinth, that there may be many "who have sinned in the past and have not repented" (changed their minds and altered their course of action) "of their unclean lives, their fornication and sensuality".[15]

The occurrence of the words may be rare in the Pauline writings. The importance of the concept of radical thinking leading to radical action is in no doubt at all.

To take another of Paul's concepts, he pleads with the Roman Christians to adapt themselves "no longer to the pattern of this present world, but let your minds be remade and your whole nature thus transformed".[16] More literally the last phrase can be translated: "Be transfigured by the renewal of the mind". The verb is used by Matthew and Mark of Jesus when he "was transfigured" before Peter, James and John.[17] Apart from these passages, it is used only once elsewhere in the New Testament, this time again by Paul – "we are transfigured into [Christ's] likeness from splendour to splendour; such is the influence of the Lord who is Spirit." In the days of Moses, Paul is pointing out, the *minds* of the Israelites were closed (2 Cor 3:14). But when a man turns to the Lord the veil is removed, his mind is renewed, he is transfigured, and the process of glorification is set in motion.[18]

The use of the mind, the process of thinking, was to Paul a matter of great importance. "As a man thinks, so he is", runs the old adage. "All that is true, all that is noble ... just and pure ... lovable and gracious ... excellent and admirable – *fill your thoughts* with these things."[19] The verb can be used of accountancy – "reckon these things among your assets": minds which move in these areas make for rich characters. A life of love and humility is most likely to emerge from meditation on the life and self-offering of Jesus who "did not think to snatch at equality with God, but made himself nothing, assuming the nature of a slave . . .".[20]

When Paul wrote: "We have the mind of Christ",[21] he was not writing boastfully or brashly. He was simply giving expression to his conviction that "those who were truly Christian had the power to discover for themselves what was the will of God, especially in matters of conduct".[22] "He trusted the educated Christian conscience to ascertain what was the will of God. And he believed that the education of conscience went on largely within the Fellowship and was mediated through its worship"[23] – "*we* have the mind", not "I" as a lonely individual, though every individual disciple will seek to "take every thought captive to obey Christ".[24]

The charge of Peter to his readers to "gird up the loins of your mind"[25] would have appealed to Paul; it is a virile concept, wholly in keeping, as we have seen, with his own way of thinking. And surely it is in keeping with our Lord's way of thinking and teaching – with his refusal to treat people as children, his insistence on answering their questions with questions of his own, his pricking of the closed or closing mind with the question: "What do you think? How does it seem to *you*?" It probably annoyed them that he refused to give them packaged answers. "If you have ears to hear, then hear." If you have minds to think, use them.

The conversion experience of Paul did not mean the diminution, still less the death, of his thinking processes and of his mental activity. The reverse was the case. Dedication to a cause – in his case dedication to Christ – heightened his faculties and gave a sharpened edge to his intellect. David Knowles, writing of Baron von Hügel, says that "the mature, old, mellow Baron . . . has, with St Augustine and so few others, both mind and heart."[26] Paul must be numbered, pre-eminently, with those "few others". In him we find a conjunction of mind and spirit, of intelligence and perception, of a very rare order. He would have been the last to play off theology against religion. He would have come down on the side of Adolf Schlatter in his attack on the notion that the New Testament contains not theology but religion. "For him, theology deals with our relation to God, which moves us *totally*. Religion is intellectual."[27]

The point is one of great importance. It is when we play off mind against heart, making a dichotomy where there should be a unity, that we run into trouble. A false emphasis on the heart can lead to sentimentality, as an exclusive stress on the mind can lead to intellectual pride and idolatry. The recent biographies of Dorothy Sayers and of Charles Darwin can be of help to us in illustrating the points at issue.

James Brabazon, in writing of Dorothy Sayers, has much to say about her almost exclusively intellectual approach to the Christian religion. "She did her best to depersonalise the whole thing by scrupulously sticking to a restatement of Church doctrine, and refusing to be drawn at any time into 'what Christ means to me' or any other form of personal avowal."[28] When Longmans approached her about writing a book on Christianity, she replied that she felt "that religious books at this moment should on no account be 'personal'".[29] Later on, she attributed her (undoubted) "irritable and domineering spirit" to the fact that "she had found herself caught up against her will in the evangelisation business".[30] There seems to have been – at least for most of her life – a dis-junction between her intellectual apprehension of the Faith and the relating of it to personal experience, her own or that of her relatives and friends. When she was at work on her very successful translation of Dante's *The Divine Comedy*, her husband, O.A. Fleming ("Mac"), died. "Dorothy", says her biographer,

> must have wondered a little, as her translation took her up the terraces of Purgatory where the repentant souls gladly endured the cauterising of their sins for the sake of the joy beyond, what exactly was happening to 'poor, dear old Mac'. It is a great lack in our understanding of Dorothy that there seems to be no indication anywhere in her writing that she was aware of any connection between the fate of those literary souls that she expounded so brilliantly, and that of this particular individual soul that she knew so well.[31]

Writing to John Wren Lewis towards the end of her life, Dorothy Sayers said:

> I am not a priest ... I am not by temperament an evangelist ... I am quite without the thing known as 'inner light' or 'spiritual experience'. I have never undergone conversion ... It follows naturally, perhaps, from this that I am quite incapable of 'religious emotion.' ... I do not know whether we can be saved through the intellect, but I do know that I can be saved by nothing else. I know that, if there is judgement, I shall have to be able to say: "This alone, Lord, in Thee and in me, have I never betrayed, and may it suffice to know and love and choose Thee after

this manner, for I have no other love, or knowledge, or choice in me."[32]

Her biographer comments: ". . . something, some self-mistrust, prevented her from ever making the connection between the dogmatic and the personal."[33]

This brief exploration into the approach of Dorothy Sayers to the Christian religion may serve to draw out more clearly the approach of Paul by way of contrast. For him, such a dis-junction between the intellectual and the experiential would have been quite unthinkable. He could not "depersonalise the whole thing by scrupulously sticking to a restatement of Church doctrine", for there was something so intimately personal about his relationship with Christ that it could only be expressed by the use of personal pronouns – "the Son of God loved me and gave himself up for me".[34] His experience of God was indissolubly connected with the depths of Christian doctrine. He was no travel agent hired to expatiate to others on the beauties of foreign countries while he himself had never stepped beyond his own native land. Paul had been there; in fact, he was already "a citizen of heaven"[35] – he tasted its joys every day. James Brabazon contrasts Dorothy Sayers' religion with that of Charles Williams – "where Dorothy expounded the laws of the spiritual world like an exceptionally brilliant law-student, Williams seemed actually to inhabit that world, and to understand in his blood and bones the truths of which the laws were merely man-made formulations. And where the only religious conviction that she could speak of from personal experience was the conviction of sin, he was aware of it all, from the depths of damnation to the height of salvation and all the highways and byways between."[36] Williams had been there. So, I repeat, had Paul.

So far from finding himself "caught up against (his) will in the evangelisation business", the very reverse was the case with the apostle. "It would be misery to me

108

not to preach" the Gospel.[37] As an ambassador, he was
at his post solely to commend the cause of his Sovereign.
An inner urgency moved him, till he found himself
saying: "In Christ's name, we implore you, be reconciled
to God!"[38] Given that evangelism is clearly understood
to have nothing to do with proselytising, given that it is
separated by a hemisphere from pressurising, then
Paul's approach would seem to have been a natural and
right one. To be able to say: "This one thing I do"[39] is to
find at the centre of one's being a liberating force which
can go far to free one from that "irritable and domineering spirit" which, in her best moments, distressed
Dorothy Sayers.

To attempt to pursue a line of separation between
mind and heart, between theology and religion, when
we are dealing with the Christian faith is to engage in a
very dangerous course of action. In the case of Dorothy
Sayers it led to her making the monstrously patronising
remark – or was she talking with her tongue in her
cheek? – "I love St Paul; he was such a fine little chap."
"Fine little chap" indeed! As well might one say, looking
at the Himalayas: "How pretty they are! Nice little
hills, those!"

Few students of the nineteenth century would question the claim that Charles Darwin possessed one of the
greatest minds of that period and that his researches
marked an epoch in the progress of human thought.
Peter Brent's biography, brought out a century after
Darwin's death, gives us the portrait of a man moved by
a passion to acquire knowledge, to unlock the secret of
the evolutionary unity of the planetary system, our own
planet, its geology, its climate, its living organisms and
their social organisations. Brent remarks on "the profound state of concentration in which he pursued his
theories . . . the all-demanding inner effort that he
called . . . the 'excessive labour of inventive thought'."[40]
"Problems in general philosophy, in theology, in political science doubtless had their interest, but it was an
interest that Darwin preferred to ignore. He had, he

insisted, only so much energy available, and this he wished to direct into those activities that really concerned him."[41] "He swiftly returned the copy of Kant's *Critique of Pure Reason* that Julia Wedgwood lent him, reporting that 'it had said nothing to him'."[42] As for the Christian religion, it was for him, like politics and sport, simply a part of his social history. "His tepid involvement with Christianity was burned away by his intense devotion to science."[43] "The Heavenly Father, never very apparent in Darwin's personal firmament, seems ... to have faded away ..."[44] and he moved towards a "quiet, undemonstrative atheism", a state in which he found himself unable to accept as truth "the obfuscations of religion".[45]

His "one-pointed" search, the vision which came to him probably most clearly on his voyage home to England on the *Beagle*, took the place of a religion in his life. *"An illuminating vision, an absorbing mental effort, a pervasive sense of certainty: the combination suggests a man seized and utterly changed by a profound inner experience."*[46] I have italicised the words, for they could have been written as perceptively and as accurately about Paul as they were written by his biographer about Charles Darwin. "Vision ... mental effort ... sense of certainty." "This one thing I do" – this "one-pointed" concentration – this binds together the agnostic (?atheistic) man of science of the nineteenth century and the profound theologian-missionary of the first. But the difference – and it is a vast difference – is that for the latter, it was a passion to know *him* in whose face he had seen the glory of God, to know *him* and the power of his resurrection, to know *him* and to share in his sufferings. Brent wrote of Darwin's "consuming motivation", of his "being driven by a passion" compared with which everything else must be "marginal to him ... *the desire to know*".[47] Every phrase here could be used of Paul, but the object of the verb "to know" must be added, and it can be none other than "Christ Jesus my Lord, for whom I have suffered the loss of all things". *There* is the difference between the two men of thought who have each of them left an indelible mark on the generations that have followed them.

Darwin's heart would have beaten no faster when he heard the words of the seventeenth-century German writer, J. Scheffler:

> Thee will I love, my strength, my tower,
> Thee will I love, my joy, my crown,
> Thee will I love with all my power,
> In all my works, and Thee alone.
> Thee will I love, till sacred fire
> Fills my whole soul with pure desire.

Paul's heart would have beaten faster and faster as the hymn went on. The "knowledge" that moved Paul was the "wisdom" of God, to many nonsense, "obfuscatory" nonsense, but to him "Christ the power of God and the wisdom of God . . . Christ Jesus, who of God is made unto us wisdom, and righteousness, and sanctification and redemption".[48] In him, mind and heart focused. Here was his point of unity.

When Paul spoke of the proclamation of Christ nailed to the cross being a stumbling-block to Jews and folly to Greeks, when he spoke of divine folly being wiser than man's wisdom, when he spoke of God shaming the wise,[49] he was not inveighing against reason as such. Bornkamm makes the point well:

> What he says about saving event and faith is not dictated by any secret delight in the absurd. He demands no 'blind' faith, and says absolutely nothing about the sacrifice of understanding and intellect. No, what the word of the cross says is that through this 'foolish' gospel God turned 'the world's wisdom' into foolishness. What characterises the latter is the desire to measure God by its own standards. It is thus shown to be man's attempt to hold his own with God.[50]

Paul was no formal theologian if, by that phrase, we mean a purely speculative thinker. But he was one of the world's deepest thinkers, whose theology was always related to life as it is, in all its beauty and all its sordidness. Pastoral issues drew out his most profound thought. He wanted every thought to be brought into captivity to the obedience of Christ;[51] for he knew from his own experience and from what he had seen in the lives of his fellow-disciples that when men's minds get to work on the ideas of Christ and when they live "after the manner of Christ Jesus",[52] "centred ... on Christ",[53] then their judgement is sound, their life and conduct wholesome. Let a community "continue ... in the unity of love", let it "come to the full wealth of conviction which understanding brings, and grasp God's secret",[54] and one need not fear for its future, however contrary the winds that blow upon it. What is most to be dreaded is a "mind *made insensitive*",[55] 'petrified'. The verb is used in classical Greek of causing a callus to be formed, and so, in the New Testament, it is used of the heart, the centre of mind and affection, becoming callous.[56]

We shall understand Paul best if we regard him not primarily as a dogmatist but as a learner intent on exploring ever more fully the depths of God, the unsearchable riches of Christ, and the love which passes knowledge. From his conversion onwards, from the day when he was freed from the old legalism, his originality found a stimulus which owed its origin and continuation to the Lord, the Spirit. A man of big mental and spiritual build, he found that now, in Christ, he had a capacity for growth that knew no limits. To pass from the servitude of the law of Moses into an ever-deepening servitude to Christ was to move into a realm of increasing liberty of mind and soul.

T. R. Glover, describing what it meant to Paul to be a "fellow-worker with Christ",[57] once wrote: "To live with an artist and to watch his touch, to catch his angle of vision, to learn at last to anticipate how his mind will work, is a supreme opportunity for any man who has an eye for greatness and truth. In no fanciful way, but literally, we may say that Paul lived so with Christ; at least it was his ideal, and the combination of such an ideal with personal love and gratitude is an incomparable training."[58] Such a man, "in momentary communication with his Captain, always ready for the signal, the hint, where to press forward, what to emphasise . . ."[59] has within him an openness to new truth and fresh insights which will not diminish but rather will increase as the years go by. Here is the answer to spiritual or mental stagnation, and Paul knew a great deal about it. Hand in hand with a deepening love of God went an increasing insight into human nature in all its complexity. Like his Master before him, of whom it was said that "he knew men so well . . . that he needed no evidence from others about a man, for he himself could tell what was in a man",[60] and like many a saint after him, Paul grew in an appreciation of men and women – how many friends he had! – and in an understanding of their spiritual needs. Something of this can be seen in the prayers which he uttered for them, and in the messages he sent to them.

We have said that "Paul was no formal theologian if, by that phrase, we mean a purely speculative thinker". We should not compare him with a St Thomas Aquinas building up his *Summa Theologica* or a Karl Barth producing, over a period of thirty years, his *Kirchliche Dogmatic* (Church Dogmatics). He cannot be called a systematic theologian in the later sense of that term. Though he had been taught his Jewish faith by experts at Tarsus and at Jerusalem, though he became a creative thinker whose works were to influence men and nations in ways far beyond his wildest imagination, the nature of his divine commission was such as to make his writings the work of a peripatetic evangelist rather than of a scholarly expert. He was a lover of souls, the pastor of a flock. His theology reflects his primary concerns, and is pastoral, passionate, warm, creative.

We may add: is not theology seen at its best when it is allied to evangelistic concern and pastoral care?

Michael Ramsey, in an address on Anselm of Bec, whom he calls "the greatest of the Archbishops of Canterbury", says that "Anselm shows how theology and pastoral care belong together." And he comments: "Nothing is sadder in our contemporary theological scene in England than the frequent growing apart of academic theology from spirituality and pastoral responsibility . . . The nature of theology itself shows that the theologian is one with the man of prayer and the pastor of souls."[61]

Certainly in Paul theology and spirituality went together, for in his letters he never tired of telling his readers how constantly he remembered them in his prayers.[62] It was precisely because he cared for his readers, and cared as a pastor, that he wrote theologically to them, for he knew that belief matters. "Every idea is hollow if it is not fleshed out in real life."[63]

The nature of Paul's theology is reflected in the character and style of his writing. A contrast may illuminate this matter. Let us look at John Henry Newman engaged on his writing work. In a letter to his biographer, Wilfrid Ward, he compared the composition of a volume to "a gestation and child-birth". He elaborated the comparison:

My book on Justification . . . I write, I write again: I write a third time in the course of six months. Then I take the third: I literally fill the paper with corrections, so that another person could not read it. I then write it out fair for the printer. I put it by; I take it up; I begin to correct again: it will not do. Alterations multiply, pages are rewritten, little lines sneak in and crawl about. The whole page is disfigured; I write again; I cannot count how many times this process is repeated.[64]

The result of this time-consuming and patient labour was to give to Newman's work a singular directness and logic of expression, and to make him "one of the greatest of English prose stylists in the nineteenth century".[65]

Now let us look at Paul. There are passages, it is true, where every word seems to be in place, and where the theme of which he writes elevates the style which he uses. Who would want to alter a word in his superb hymn to love in 1 Corinthians 13, or in the passage in which he expresses his conviction about the love of God in Christ Jesus at the end of the eighth chapter of the Epistle to the Romans, or in the doxology which concludes chapter eleven of that letter? How did he do it? Did he sit down as Newman sat (or, rather, stood at his high desk), and weigh up every word, altering this and adding that? Or did the subject so possess him, so overwhelm him, that he was lifted to a higher plane and enabled to write what, for sheer power and beauty, must have surprised him as much as his readers, when he came to read it in the cool light of later reflection? I suspect the process was more one of 'inspiration' than of laboured writing and re-writing.

When we come to look at his letters as a whole, we do not get the impression of a Newman-like attention to detail. On the contrary, his style is often staccato, explosive, untidy. He embarks on a theme and then – an idea strikes him and he is off on a huge parenthesis. Let me illustrate: the reader of Ephesians 3, verse 1, has to wait until verse 14 for the verb whose subject "I, Paul" has been set out at the beginning of the chapter! What has happened? The mention of "you Gentiles" in verse 1 has sparked off a theme in the apostle's mind which he cannot delay developing. So verses 2 to 13 are devoted to the enthralling subject of the inclusion of Gentiles in God's master-plan along with Jews, and the reader has to wait in patience until verse 14 to be told what it is that Paul prays for his readers.

Again, the Epistle to the Galatians is difficult to the modern reader largely because it bears the marks of

115

having been dashed off by a writer in the heat of his concern, and even of his anger – here is a writer who could not stay to polish the style or to tie up the broken ends of his Greek. In this respect, it corresponds to the prophecy of Hosea, where the suffering and pathos of the writer are reflected in the raggedness of his Hebrew. Galatians is a stormy letter whose writer cannot stay to deploy his argument in the more leisurely way that he does in the Epistle to the Romans, where some of the same issues are being considered. If there is harshness in Galatians, it is the harshness of a shepherd defending his sheep when wolves are at their throat, and it is combined with an almost womanly tenderness and a perplexity about them which gives rise to a rebuke tempered by a touch of humour – dear, silly idiots that they are![66]

Often, of course, he writes against the background of assumptions which the readers fully understood but which we, reading the letters at a distance of space and time, cannot fully appreciate. It is clear that a large part of the first Epistle to the Corinthians is, in fact, a reply to questions which the readers had sent to the apostle for answer. He says so clearly in 7: 1 – "now for the matters you wrote about." We may note also – "on the question of celibacy"; "about food consecrated to heathen deities"; "about eating this consecrated food"; "about gifts of the Spirit"; "about the collection in aid of God's people".[67] His first readers understood much more than we do about the circumstances behind the asking of these questions. They wrestled with the problems daily. We have to fill in the background as best we may.

There are passages, fortunately few in number, where Paul uses a kind of exposition of the Old Testament text or of an incident recorded in the Old Testament, which would have been common in the circles of Rabbinic learning in which Paul was at home, but which are quite foreign to our modern methods of understanding Scripture. Such a passage is the one

116

about "the covenant that comes from Mount Sinai: that is Hagar."[68] Here Paul uses the allegorical method of exposition, loved by Philo and the Alexandrian school of exegetes. He uses it again in a passage in which the story of the journey of the children of Israel through the Red Sea is allegorised in such a way as to make it refer to the Christian sacrament of baptism.[69] And there is a third instance where Paul refers to the kindly law of the Old Testament which forbade the muzzling of an ox while he was doing threshing work.[70] "Do you suppose", he asks, "that God's concern is with oxen?" He knew perfectly well that it *was*. He goes on: "Or is the reference clearly to ourselves? Of course it refers to us . . ." and he proceeds to point the moral that a Christian worker deserves a proper material reward for services rendered![71] To us, such biblical interpretation seems perverse, and it is with an effort that we put ourselves into the position of the Rabbis one of whose tenets was that "God could say many things at the same time". We have only to read the highly fanciful exegesis of many early writers to be thankful that Paul used the allegorical method as rarely as he did.

Then we must bear in mind that the apostle sometimes – we do not know how often – used a scribe. No doubt it was a high privilege to be the secretary to so rare a soul, but the task must have presented formidable difficulties! "I Tertius, who took this letter down"[72] must have sometimes wished that his employer did not *talk* his letters, and that his mind did not sweep on so rapidly from one concept to another, did not sometimes hint at an idea and leave the reader to develop it, did not fail to give the amanuensis a chance to get the words down before he was off on some other flight of exploration or thanksgiving.

If we are honest, however, we must admit that the greatest difficulty which we encounter in coming to grips with the writings of Paul consists in the fact that he was a giant – intellectually and spiritually – and we are small men compared with him. We cannot be surprised if there is strain when ordinariness meets genius.

> Why, man, he doth bestride the narrow world
> Like a Colossus; and we petty men
> Walk under his huge legs, and peep about
> To find ourselves dishonourable graves.
> Men at some time are masters of their fates:
> The fault, dear Brutus, is not in our stars,
> But in ourselves, that we are underlings.[73]

The fault, dear reader, is not in Paul – at least, not always! – but in the paucity of our spiritual life. Shallow will not answer to deep.

However, to realise that, in reading the Pauline literature, we are in the company of a great Christian is in itself a healthy experience, if a heady one.

> The intellectual range of his gospel ... soared to incomparable heights – today still unconquered. Small wonder that many readers are left gasping at his letters – loaded to the line with a heavy cargo of thought – and that not a few who yield themselves to his gospel are left feeling like a traveller overcome by vertigo in an Alpine region surrounded by steep, cloud-covered peaks, who often does not know how to follow on and how he is going to last the journey.[74]

Paul, thinker and writer, has an uncomfortable way of challenging our spiritual and intellectual littleness.

MAN OF PRAYER

Prayer goeth up, pity cometh down.
God's grace is richer than prayer: God always giveth
more than he is asked.
The prayer of the humble pierceth the clouds.
Prayer is colloquy with God.

> Lancelot Andrewes: *Preces Privatae*

A person who is too busy to pray will also be too busy to
think; and what is the good of labour that is not guided
by constant thought about its meaning and its end?
Prayer, after all, is but thinking towards God.

> John Baillie: *Christian Devotion*

Never give up prayer, thank God for everything . . .

> 1 Thessalonians 5: 17,18 (Moffatt)

MAN OF PRAYER

That prayer occupied a central, dominating place in the life of Paul is clear from even a superficial reading of his letters. As the son of a devout Jewish family, Saul had, of course, been nurtured in a religion of prayer. The worship of the synagogue was itself based on the great tradition of the Psalms – they were its prayer-book, the primary source on which the Jewish people drew in the creation of their later liturgy. Doubtless he could never be thankful enough for those Psalms, that liturgy, that synagogue, and that "temple worship" of which he spoke with such reverence in his letter to the Romans.[1]

But his prayer-life as a Christian was based on something more than this. Its foundation was that of a new relationship with God in Christ, the like of which he had not known in the days of his Pharisaic orthodoxy. It was not so much a contrast as a fulfilment, as a full-grown flower is the fulfilment of a bud. To change that metaphor, the prayers which he had been taught in his youth formed the foundation of the building of his spiritual life – a very good and noble foundation. But the building erected on that foundation was something more wonderful than anything he had been able to conceive of before it rose.

In his synagogue days he had indeed been able to think of himself as part of the family of which God was the Father. But now in Christ that Fatherhood took on a new, more intimate meaning. It began with his conversion-baptism experience which he described so vividly in his letters. The life of fear was left behind – no more slavery! He could now cry out with his fellow-Christians "Abba! Father!" He had within him the witness of the

Spirit that he, with them, was a child of God. That must have had as a necessary, though almost unbelievable, consequence, that he was an heir to immense spiritual wealth; and that in turn meant that he shared his heir-ship with Christ himself. We note the progress outlined in these verses – sons, heirs, fellow-heirs with Christ, sharers in his sufferings now and in his splendour hereafter.[2]

The highest privilege of sonship is the right of free access to and intimacy with the father, the sharing by a son with his father in the latter's experience, thinking and planning. No hindrance to entry, but freedom of access – this is at the very heart of the meaning of sonship.

The word "access" (*prosagōgē*) occurs three times in the New Testament – the first in the letter to the Romans: through Christ "we have access by faith into this grace wherein we stand".[3] Some have seen a nautical nuance here, "grace" being the haven, and "access" the "approach", as of a boat to a harbour. The other two references are in the letter to the Ephesians.[4]

The first of these two is trinitarian in form – "through *him* (Christ) we both alike (Jew and Gentile) have access to the *Father* in the one *Spirit*." In recent years, there has been a certain neglect of the doctrine of the blessed Trinity in much thinking and writing. Much has been written about the second Person of the Trinity – his nature and work; and in popular religion we have all been made aware of the Jesus people. After a long barren period of neglect, the Holy Spirit has come alive, if we may so use the phrase, in doctrine and experience. Our shelves are full of books, some worthy, some unworthy, about the third Person of the Trinity, and our hymnology has been enlarged and (sometimes) enriched by poetry which is charismatic. But it is high time that we thought more and spoke more about Father, Son and Holy Spirit in the mystery and fullness of their unity. We may note a remark of Nils Alstrup Dahl: "Whereas a number of major works and monographs deal with Christology, . . . it is hard to find any comprehensive or penetrating study of the theme 'God in the New Testament'."[5] And we may be thankful to Thomas A. Smail for providing us with a book whose deeply significant title is *The Forgotten Father*. It is a timely attempt to set right, in theology and experience, a certain imbalance which has begun to imperil fullness of doctrine and practice. He writes:

> Out of his relationship to his Father Jesus found the strength and obedience for all his living and dying; to him we have to look for definition of both God's fatherhood and our sonship. But it is the business of the Holy Spirit to take the things of Jesus and open them up to us, so that we in our way become participant in them. That is the basis of all the particular charismata, the gifts of grace. And it is also the basis of this central gift of grace, that the *Spirit opens up to us the holy of holies and bids us enter,* and become sharers in Jesus' relationship to the Father. At the springs of our being, deeper than emotion or even intellect, although moving and informing both, he cries to us and in our fear and unbelief convinces us that the Father of Jesus is our father too.[6]

Paul reverts to this subject of access to God: "In him (Christ) we have access to God with freedom, in the confidence born of trust in him."[7] This passage is not trinitarian in the sense that the former passage is, but the note of confidence is struck here as it is not there. The word translated 'freedom' in the New English Bible is translated 'boldness' in the Authorised Version in this verse. Its primary meaning is freedom or boldness *of speech*, outspokenness, though often it is used with a more general meaning of joyful confidence. Here, in the context of our access to God in Christ, we may detect a hint of both meanings: we may approach God with a joyful confidence which will naturally result in a freedom of speech with him such as characterises the speech of a son on good terms with his father. Elsewhere in the Pauline writings, the word 'boldness' is used of the apostle's approach to his fellow-humans.[8] Here it is used of a believer's approach to God, and it reminds us of the way in which the writer of the Epistle to the Hebrews speaks – "let us *boldly* approach the throne of our gracious God"; "the blood of Jesus makes us free to enter *boldly* into the sanctuary . . ."[9] This is not the storming of the gates of an unwilling deity. Nor, on the other hand, does it suggest a hand-shaking familiarity. This is the quiet, steady confidence of a son who can speak freely with his father, thereby sharing his experience, his thinking, his planning. The author of the first Epistle of John writes in similar vein: "If our conscience does not condemn us, then we can approach God with confidence".[10] If that note is often strangely lacking in personal and public prayer today, the writers of the New Testament cannot be blamed for our reticence!

Within the body of Paul's writings, there are two passages in which a specially strong light is cast on what prayer meant to the apostle in his own experience. The first comes in his second letter to the Corinthians.[11] He writes, as it were, anonymously. He stands outside himself (that is the root meaning of 'ecstasy'), and looks at himself, at the revelation which came to him, and at the outcome which made so profound a difference to his life. He does so with a kind of detachment – "I know a Christian man . . . I know that this same man . . . was caught up into paradise . . ." That does not diminish the authenticity of what he writes; it even enhances it. The great violinist Kreisler once said: "I think a player must be in a certain state himself to be able to make anyone else feel what he is interpreting. If the player himself does not change his usual state, he will be able to convey nothing to those who are listening. This state is analogous to trance. The nervous system is toned up, the brain becomes clearer, the feelings more sensitive." A more modern speaker might talk in terms of an extra secretion of adrenalin when he plays, acts, preaches; but we know what he means.

A vision, a revelation, it was indeed. Yet it had to do with a very mundane matter. There is nothing much more mundane than a thorn in the flesh, a sharp stake which pierces and hurts. But that very painful experience proved to be Paul's meeting place with God, providing him with an experience of grace in the midst of distress, and teaching him lessons which he could have learned in no other way.

In similar style, nineteen centuries later, Edward Woods, Bishop of Lichfield, broadcasting over the BBC and speaking in the third person, told of his own painful experience and of its outcome:

> I know a man who, some time ago, had a serious breakdown in health and was obliged to go abroad for some years. It meant the break-up of his home, the abandonment of useful and interesting work, and the future looked black. On the Channel crossing he found running in his head the title of one of Tolstoy's tales, 'Things Men Live By'; and he wondered if his present disaster was one of the things he had to learn to live by. In the event he found that it was so. The thing took indeed a lot of learning, and there were kicks against the pricks; but the time did come when he could honestly thank God for what had at first seemed sheer calamity.[12]

The second passage which casts light on what prayer meant to Paul in his own experience is in the eighth chapter of the Epistle to the Romans.[13] This passage can only be properly understood if it is studied in the context of the paragraphs which precede it. From verse 12 onwards one of the main themes is that of sonship – "it is those who are driven" (the word is the same as that used of *the* Son of God in Luke 4) "by the Spirit of God who are sons of God" (v.14). These are the people who, released from slavery and fear, can cry out "Abba,

125

Father" (v.15). These are the people who (as we saw earlier) are fellow-heirs with Christ, sharing in his suffering now and his splendour hereafter (v.17). These are the people for whose revealing the whole created universe waits with eager anticipation (v.19). But until that revealing takes place, until God's plan reaches its consummation, the redeemed, God's sons though they are, share their lot with a creation which "groans and travails" (v.22 ff.). They, too, suffer weakness and the inability to know what rightly to pray for (v.26), an inability which at times leaves them speechless before God. All they can manage is wordless groans.

Such a situation might suggest that prayer is useless – why continue if words fail? It is at this point that Paul's experience of the Holy Spirit rescues him from despair and gives him an understanding of what prayer really is. As Friedrich Heiler puts it: "Prayer is not man's work, or discovery or achievement, but *God's* work in man."[14] At the point of our greatest weakness, our inability, our wordlessness, the Holy Spirit comes to "lend us a hand". (The verb in v.26 is only used elsewhere in the New Testament in the story where Martha, hot and distracted, asks Jesus to bid Mary "come and lend a hand" in the kitchen!)[15] As an infant, seeking to make its needs known, can only cry wordlessly but the mother understands, so a man or woman at prayer finds his wordless groans taken up by the Spirit and interpreted into the ears of the Father, and the Father "co-operates for good with those who love him". So Professor G. W. H. Lampe writes: "At a very deep level of human personality God's Spirit interacts with the spirit of man in prayer. This is made possible because the initiative in prayer is taken by God and does not depend on human ability and effort."[16]

Such is the work of the *Spirit* in relation to the believer's praying. But we find that Paul asserts that *Christ* intercedes for us, "pleads our cause".[17] To quote Lampe again: "It is . . . difficult, despite Paul's belief in Christ as a personal contemporary reality, to be clear how far he really distinguishes this 'Christ' in practice from the Spirit of God. Often 'Christ' and 'Spirit' are functionally identified . . ."[18] The beginnings of that difficulty are to be found in the writings of Paul; and this is by no means the only passage in his letters where the work of Christ and that of the Holy Spirit are so close as to be virtually incapable of differentiation.

Christ "pleads our cause". To translate this word as "intercedes" is to run the danger of misunderstanding. Bishop Michael Ramsey has pointed out that

> the Greek verb does not properly mean to speak or to plead or to make petitions or entreaties; it means rather to be with someone, to meet or encounter someone, in relation to others. What is called the intercession of Jesus means his ceaseless presence with the Father. He is with the Father not as begging the Father to be gracious, for from the Father graciousness ever flows. He is with the Father as one who died for us on Calvary; with the Father in the presence of a life which is ever, the life that died; with the Father as one who was tempted as we are and bore our sins and our sufferings; with the Father as the focus of our hopes and desires.[19]

Praying, from this point of view, is being consciously in Christ in the presence of the Father. Here *words* are of comparative unimportance.

In this, Michael Ramsey is very close to Bishop B. F. Westcott who, commenting on Hebrews 7: 25, writes that Christ's "very presence before God in His humanity is in itself a prevailing intercession". He goes on: "In the Levitical ritual the truth was foreshadowed in the direction that 'Aaron shall bear the names of the children of Israel in the breastplate of judgement upon his heart when he goeth in unto the holy place . . .' (Exod. 28: 29)."[20]

Professor E. Allison Peers in his study of St John of the Cross says: "It would be a very insensitive reader who failed to realise that the Saint is writing, not of what he has gathered from books, but of what he has himself experienced."[21] Precisely the same could be said of Paul in relation to the subject of prayer. As I have written elsewhere: "His own experience of God in Christ, his own experience of prayer, was the soil out of which his prayer-life grew. This he shared with his hearers and readers, partly by telling them what in fact he prayed for them, partly by autobiographical hints, partly by exhortation."[22] In his letters he draws aside the veil and lets us see what prayer meant to him as he set about it in the context of a life of immense activity, frequent conflicts and heavy burdens.

Such was his experience of Christ and such his estimate of his person and work that Paul not only attributed divine functions sometimes to God and sometimes to Jesus – he could speak of the "Kingdom of God" *or* "of his Son", the "Church of God" *or* "the Church of Christ", and so on – but he also *prayed* to Jesus as to God. *Marana tha*, "our Lord, come"[23], looks like being a very early prayer of the Aramaic-speaking Church, and Paul took it over, orthodox monotheistic Jew that he was, without a tremor. "The Christological implications of this are obvious. As Moule drily comments, 'One does not call upon a mere Rabbi, after his death, to come'."[24] The Damascus road experience of Christ, pondered on in the Arabian desert, worked out in the rough and tumble of his missionary labours, had given him One to whom at every turn of the road he could pray in the confidence that he was heard and understood.

The language Paul used, when writing about prayer, is highly suggestive. He liked to speak about "making mention of", or "remembering" his friends in his intercessions.[25] Often, no doubt, he was perplexed as to what precisely was their need or what particularly were the difficulties in which they found themselves. That mattered little. It was enough to mention their names before the Lord – silently to hold them up, as it were, in the divine presence. "Lord, there is young John in

Philippi, old Anna in Ephesus, busy Andrew in Colossae, tempted Tertius in Galatia. Oh, and I must not forget . . ." So the mentioning went on, and John and Anna and Andrew and Tertius wondered why there seemed to come to them a new accretion of strength and spiritual vigour; they had forgotten that Paul had been doing his "mentioning" work, his remembering of them.

> The weary ones had rest, the sad had joy
> That day and wondered how.
> A ploughman singing at his work had prayed
> "Lord help them now".
>
> Away in foreign lands they wondered how
> Their simple words had power.
> At home the Christians, two and three, had met
> To pray an hour.
>
> Yes, we are always wondering, wondering how,
> Because we do not see
> Someone, unknown perhaps and far away,
> On bended knee.

In his autobiography, Harry Williams speaks of intercession as being "like putting myself at their disposal before God", and he adds the significant point that in intercession "we shall find ourselves identified with a fair degree of suffering, adding to what may be our own sufferings the sufferings of those others . . . To intercede for people is to be willing . . . to share their hurt so that it is felt to lie on our shoulders as well as theirs."[26]

It is in this context that we should consider the meaning of Paul's favourite phrase "without ceasing".[27] How could such a busy man as he pray unceasingly? For that matter, how could he expect his readers to? They had far too many things to see to, things perfectly legitimate, which demanded their care and full attention. The quick breathing of a name, the momentary mention, is all that is needed, and the Father hears.

The linking of prayer with thanksgiving added a note

of joy to the apostle's prayer-work.[28] No doubt he often found, as many others have done, that thanksgiving 'primed the pump' of prayer when he felt least inclined to pray.

But it was best of all, and most important of all, to remember that real prayer is prayer "in the Spirit".[29] C. S. Lewis makes the point that "prayer in its most perfect state is a soliloquy. If the Holy Spirit speaks in the man, then in prayer 'God speaks to God'."[30] He quotes a poem (anonymously, but actually it was by himself) to which Paul would have given his assent:

> They tell me, Lord, that when I seem
> To be in speech with you,
> Since but one voice is heard, it's all a dream,
> One talker aping two.
>
> Sometimes it is, yet not as they
> Conceive it. Rather, I
> Seek in myself the things I hoped to say,
> But lo! my wells are dry.
>
> Then, seeing me empty, you forsake
> The listener's role and through
> My dumb lips breathe and into utterance wake
> The thoughts I never knew.
>
> And thus you neither need reply
> Nor can; thus, while we seem
> Two talkers, thou art One for ever, and I
> No dreamer, but thy dream.

To put it another way, the Christian at prayer always has, wonderfully available,

> a Holy Spirit's energies,
> An Advocate with God.[32]

This approach to prayer accounts for the sense of awe which we detect when Paul writes about the subject, awe which must always be in evidence when the finite comes into the presence of the Infinite. It also accounts for the sense of filial confidence, even of intimacy, which we have noticed to be a mark of Paul at prayer. The two are not incompatible. Awe and confidence are the two sides of a coin of immense value. Paul grasped that value, and longed to share it with his followers.

FREEDOM-FIGHTER

Christ set us free, to be free men. Stand firm, then . . .
Galatians 5: 1

I have strength for anything through him who gives me power.
Philippians 4: 13

Religion is grace, and ethics is gratitude.
Thomas Erskine: *Letters*

We should not shrink from trying to work within the structures of society in order to shift them. We are not called to drop out entirely into an alternative world . . . We have to build from the bottom up at the same time as we think about reshaping the whole framework.
Simon Barrington-Ward: *C.M.S. News Letter* (June, 1983)

FREEDOM-FIGHTER

The fact that Paul's missionary activity brought liberation to the members of the churches which he founded or visited, and the fact that his letters have brought a similar liberation to many who have read them, is due to Paul's own liberation of personality which he experienced in Christ. "Where the Spirit of the Lord is, there is liberty."[1] This was to Paul not the enunciation of a theory but the declaration of a fact which he was finding to be true in his own person.

The Epistle to the Galatians, probably the earliest of his letters, for all the raggedness of its literary form and in spite of at least two passages where the exegesis is, to any Gentile mind, extremely difficult, is given to the subject of liberation. It is in large part, especially its first two chapters, autobiographical and experiential. Here in Paul we see a writer to whom, it is true, God's law from one point of view had been a source of delight, but from another had been a source of bondage and condemnation. To the basic ten commandments had been added an immense super-structure of detail – the scribes had 'fenced' the Law[2] with so many rules and regulations that the observance of them proved to be a burden heavy to be borne. The more conscientious and meticulous a man was, the heavier the burden seemed to be. It became a "law of sin and death".[3] There was a judgement to come, and who was to say, for all a devout Jew's belief in the mercy of God, how the scales would tilt? Could he be right with God on a basis of his own achievements? Or was there another way?

If this matter seems to the modern reader to be about a controversy now as dead as the dodo, on further consideration it may be seen to be terribly up-to-date and relevant to modern man. A. M. Hunter put it this way:

> Ask many a modern man what Christianity means to him, and his answer will not be unlike the Pharisee's in Christ's parable (Luke 18: 9–14): "I keep the Ten Commandments – or most of them. I'm not a thief or an adulterer. I don't cheat in business or injure other people. I may not observe Lent or tithe my income for support of the church. But I respect religion – why, I even go to Holy Communion twice a year. So I'm quite happy with my little code of rules, and at the Last Judgement – if there is one – I don't think the Almighty will have much against me." Is not this, basically, the modern version of salvation by works – a few works at any rate? If Paul were among us today, would he not so have described it?[4]

It was only when Paul came to be a man in Christ that he found the resolution of this problem.

The heart-rending question which he uttered near the end of the seventh chapter of the Epistle to the Romans – "Miserable creature that I am, who is there to rescue me out of this body doomed to death?" – found a triumphant answer: "God alone, through Jesus Christ our Lord! Thanks be to God!"[5] No wonder, then, that, having faced this problem and found its answer in Christ, he wrote with passion to the Galatians: "What Christ has done is to set us free. Stand firm, then, and refuse to be tied to the yoke of slavery again."[6] "I have been crucified with Christ: the life I now live is not my life, but the life which Christ lives in me; and my present bodily life is lived by faith in the Son of God, who loved me and gave himself up for me."[7] A man who can write such words as these has found the key to a freedom which is life-enhancing. Commenting on this passage Harry Williams says in his autobiography: ". . . it doesn't in any way involve an absorption or annihilation of individual personal identity. On the contrary, individual personal identity is thus confirmed in its fullness. The saints have shown us that a man is never so fully himself as when it is not he who lives but God who lives in him."[8] John summed it up perfectly: "If then the Son sets you free, you will indeed be free."[9]

Paul saw that the key to this liberation of personality was love. "The law of the Spirit has set you free from the law of sin and death", he wrote to the Romans.[10] And to the Galatians: "The whole law can be summed up in a single commandment: 'Love your neighbour as yourself.'"[11] That love had been shed abroad in Paul's heart by the Holy Spirit given to him.[12] The one-time barren dykes of his heart had been flooded by that gift of love, and overflowed in love and goodness to others. Fully integrated himself, he was able to speak with understanding and compassion to those who as yet had not entered into his secret. And when, in his writings, he passed from the elucidation of doctrine to the presentation of ethics, he wrote as one who himself was tasting the joys of freedom and love. His ethics were those of a liberated man.

We must not look to Paul for a *system* of ethics any more than we look to him for a system of theology.[13] His ethical teaching was drawn out of him by the exigencies of his pastoral and evangelistic work. A particular pastoral situation or a set of tragic circumstances gave rise to what he wrote about sex or litigation or money or whatever. For himself his ethics had something of a unity, for they were held together by his one consuming ambition – "to be well-pleasing to Christ".[14] That was for him the touchstone by which all action was to be tested; and no doubt he longed that that should be the touchstone by which the actions of all his followers should likewise be tested. "Be followers of me, as I also am of Christ."[15]

How this is spelt out we can see in the contrast which he drew between "the works of the flesh" and "the fruit of the Spirit".[16] There is nothing in common between "the kind of behaviour which belongs to the lower nature" and "the harvest of the Spirit". The former has to do with that which gratifies the self, pandering to its desires; the latter deals with that which makes for beauty of character and issues in selfless relationships with others.

The list of qualities which constitute "the harvest of the Spirit" is of major importance. The rest of Paul's ethical teaching may be regarded as the working out, in specific detail and in particular circumstances, of what he here enumerates. Understand the meaning of these nine words – "love, joy, peace, patience, kindness, goodness, fidelity, gentleness, and self-control" and we have the key which unlocks the ethical treasury of a liberated man in Christ.

But before we examine these words one by one, we note that the apostle described the nine qualities under one all-embracing word "fruit"; not "fruits", as it is so often mis-quoted, but "fruit". "Harvest" or "crop" is a good translation, for it suggests the unity of character which may be expected to follow when the Spirit is acknowledged as Lord and proves to be the Life-giver. The "works of the flesh" are many and are totally disruptive; the "harvest of the Spirit" unifies. (Incidentally, we may note that the use of this agricultural metaphor seems to have been a favourite one in the teaching of Jesus, as for example, when he warned about false prophets recognisable for what they are "by the fruits they bear",[17] when he gave the parable of the sower (which is really the parable of the soils)[18] and the parable of the fig-tree which produced no fruit.)[19]

Further, this 'harvest' is 'of the *Spirit*', not primarily the result of human striving. It is the outcome of a man's openness to the activity within him of the Spirit of Jesus. If a man truly desires this harvest, if he seeks it with his whole heart, then he shall have it. Thomas Merton tells of a conversation which he had with Robert Lax, one of his closest friends in New York:

Merton: "How do you expect me to become a saint?"
Lax: "By wanting to."
Merton: "I can't be a saint, I can't be a saint . . ."
Lax: "All that is necessary to be a saint is to want to be one. Don't you believe that God will make you what he created you to be, if you will consent to let him do it? All you have to do is desire it."[20]

"My soul is athirst for God"[21] – that is the attitude of a person desiring the harvest of the Spirit, desiring to be a saint, to do God's will, and to be what God created him to be. Henri Nouwen tells the story of a professor who came to a Zen master to ask about Zen. The master served tea. He poured the visitor's cup full, and kept on pouring. The professor watched till he could restrain himself no longer. "It is over-full," he said. "No more will go in." "Like this cup," said the master, "you are full of your own opinions and speculations. How can I teach you Zen unless you first empty your cup?"[22]

We turn now, to look at each of the nine parts of the harvest of the Spirit.[23] Some will call for a measure of elaboration; others can be dealt with more summarily.

(i) Love
We shall see later something of the dominating place which love held in the life and thought of Paul.[24] This, however, must be said at this point. The occurrence of the word *agape (love)* is very rare outside the New Testament. It would seem that with the coming of Jesus, with the events connected with Bethlehem, Nazareth and Calvary, something so new, so radiant, had burst into the world that the words which hitherto had been used to express 'love' (*eros, philia,* etc.) now looked dull, even soiled, beside it. A new word must be found to express it. The old coinage was dim, effete. A new mintage was called for.

What are we trying to express when we speak of *agape*? Bishop Stephen Neill has described it as "the set of the will for the eternal welfare of another". That is a definition which has about it several points of value, in so far as it refers to the outworking of God's love within a person. "The set of the *will*" emphasises that Christian love is concerned primarily with the volitional rather than with the emotional part of one's make-up. So it is possible to love a person whom, naturally, one does not like, though it should be added that, when real love is at work, it is more than probable that the lover will soon see something likeable in the beloved. "Where there is no love, put love in and you will draw love out" – so said St John of the Cross.[25] There is a touch of steel about New Testament *agape*, and not one whit of the sentimental.

"The set of the will for the *eternal* welfare of another." The adjective should be noted, for it introduces the dimension of eternity. My fellow human beings are, like me, *in via*. Like me, they are trainees for heaven. There must, therefore, be an eschatological element in my relationship with them. Or, to put it more simply, it should be my concern for them, as for myself, that at the end of the journey, it should not merely be said that a good time was had by all, but rather that I had so lived and acted towards them that their eternal welfare was advanced and that they were being fashioned after the likeness of God's Son.

Such love will necessarily involve an entering into the passion, the compassion, of God; it will be costly. The biblical writers were not afraid to speak of God in ways which implied his suffering. "As a father has compassion on his children, so has the Lord compassion on all who fear him"[26] – that is a costly compassion, as any earthly father will know. "When Israel was a boy, I loved him," Hosea depicts God as saying; "I called my son out of Egypt; but the more I called, the further they went from me . . . It was I who taught Ephraim to walk, I who had taken them in my arms; but they did not know that I harnessed them in leading-strings and led them with bonds of love – that I had lifted them like a little

child to my cheek, that I had bent down to feed them."[27]
Such dereliction of the Beloved by the loved involves
heart-break, and in that sense we may rightly speak of
the passibility of God.[28] Into this suffering love Christians must enter – and enter as those who share in the
sin which grieves the heart of a holy and loving God.
Henri Nouwen rightly speaks of "a compassion that
comes out of a deep experience of solidarity, in which
one recognises that the evil, sin and violence which one
sees in the world and in the other, are deeply rooted in
one's own heart."[29]

We must, further, remark that there is an aspect of
New Testament *agape*, enjoined by Christ and underlined by Paul,[30] which often goes unnoticed but is of
considerable importance. We refer to a man's love of
himself – "love your neighbour *as yourself*". To do so
is to accept ourselves as we are, not to try to force
ourselves into another mould. To do so is not to lapse
into self-indulgence, but to enter into a new freedom; to
accept ourselves, warts and all, and not to wallow in a
morass of guilt. It is "to put up with ourselves in charity
and try to rule ourselves as we should like to rule
others", as the Abbé de Tourville used to counsel his
disciples. "What I am asking you, in the name of our
Lord, is to have charity towards yourself."

(ii) Joy
It is a matter of interest, perhaps of some surprise, that
the word 'joy' does not appear in the Synoptic Gospels in
connection with the person of Jesus. Surprise, because
surely he who was indeed "a man of sorrows and ac-
quainted with grief" must also have been a man of
manifold joys, else he would not have gathered round
him so readily a band of young men as his devoted
followers or taken such delight in nature and in little
children. The nearest that the Synoptic writers get to
ascribing joy expressly to Jesus comes in the passage
where Luke describes the return of the seventy-two

from their missionary journey and adds: "At that moment Jesus *exulted* in the Holy Spirit".[31]

John, however, who had pondered for long years on the person of Christ, makes him speak of "a joy which is (characteristically) my own",[32] and in the great High-Priestly prayer records him as interceding for his friends that "they may have my joy within them in full measure".[33]

It is surely unlikely that he who gave to the world the series of beatitudes with which Matthew begins the Sermon on the Mount[34] should have given the impression of being anything other than a happy man. For the beatitudes were a series of exclamations in the Aramaic which Jesus spoke – "oh the happiness of the poor . . . of those who mourn . . . of those of a gentle spirit . . . Rejoice, and be exceeding glad . . .!" In his own person he reflected the blessedness, the delicate gaiety, of one characterised by the features described in that Sermon. Poor Swinburne could hardly have got it more wrong when he wrote of Jesus:

> Thou hast conquered, O pale Galilean,
> The world has grown grey from thy breath.

When we turn to the writings of Paul, the picture is clear. The noun 'joy' and the verb 'to rejoice' describe a central concept in his letters. And small wonder! In the Jewish religion in which he had been brought up there was much joy. We note the Psalmists' delight in the law of the Lord,[35] and the sheer joy of a celebration such as is described by the writer in Deuteronomy[36] (including the spending of money on "cattle or sheep, wine or strong drink, or whatever you desire", but always "before the Lord", that is to say, as he approves and to his glory). Paul was the heir of a religion which had a considerable element of celebration at its heart. But also – and this was by far the greatest reason for his joy – he was living in the after-glow of the Resurrection and of Pentecost. How could such a man be other than a man of deep and lasting joy? In his list which we are considering, joy comes second only to love.

Christianity is a celebratory religion, and it is right that its central act of worship should be regarded as its supreme manifestation of joy. We *celebrate* the Eucharist. The sacrament of the word, too, should be a celebratory occasion and the sermon an act of glad thanksgiving on the part of preacher and congregation, for in the pulpit a man of the Resurrection shares with other sons and daughters of the Resurrection in celebrating the mighty acts of God in Christ.

The Church down the ages has, at its best, been a celebratory Body. It is recorded of St John of the Cross that on one occasion he took the bambino from the Christmas crib and, out of sheer joy, danced with it in his arms. Dante wrote exultingly of "the Love which moves the sun and the other stars".[37] And Catherine of Siena "shouted for joy at the sight of the earth covered with red flowers, or the milling life of an ant-heap. Everything our Creator has made is equally wonderful. 'These tiny ants have proceeded from his thought just as much as I, it caused him just as much trouble to create the angels as the animals and the flowers on the trees.'"[38] The Roman Catholic Church has been right in insisting that no one can be canonised until *hilaritas* has been proved; and G. K. Chesterton must have commended its wisdom when he remarked that it was by the force of *gravity* that Satan fell! Indeed, he ended his book *Orthodoxy* by suggesting that the gigantic secret of Christianity was humour, a joyful gaiety and mirth shared by Christ himself. Man's two special gifts which mark him off from the animals were that he is an artist (a creator) and that he laughs.

In the writings of Paul we find that, as with love, so with joy, emotion is not primary. Joy has nothing to do with a hearty back-slapping. Rather it springs from, and is the outward and visible sign of, rightness with God; it is because "we have been allowed to enter the sphere of God's grace, where we now stand" that we can

143

"exult in the hope of the divine splendour that is to be ours".[39] The roots of Christian joy go down deep into the soil of our doctrine of God and his grace.

It is perhaps at first glance surprising that *hope* finds no place in the list in Galatians 5 which we are considering. For hope is one of the great trio in Paul's hymn to love – "there are three things that last for ever: faith, hope, and love";[40] and we find the trio re-appearing in such a passage as this – ". . . your faith has shown itself in action, your love in labour, and your hope of our Lord Jesus Christ in fortitude".[41] But on further consideration it is not so surprising. For much of joy springs from anticipation and results from hope; much joy is anticipatory. The anticipation of a summer holiday gives a lift to a person during a long winter; the hope of meeting a loved one enables a man to endure the loneliness of separation and fills his heart with joy.

The joy of expectation is a large part of Christian joy – in *this* life. What "surprises of the Spirit" (to use a phrase much loved by Cardinal Suenens) await us each day, new experiences of God, new discoveries of truth, new opportunities of service? Henri Nouwen is right when he boldly declares that "a man or woman without hope in the future cannot live creatively in the present".[42] And the joy of expectation *in the life to come* is essential, too, in the thinking of Paul. "What I should like is to depart and be with Christ; that is better by far" – this is not the jaded statement of a man disillusioned by life in the present. Far from it. In the here and now he participates in a quality of living which is supernatural – "to me life is Christ". That is supremely good. But ahead there is something even better, and the apostle anticipates it with a deep joy.[43]

Finally, we may note that there is nothing escapist about joy. It is possible to exult in our present sufferings because they can prove fruitful in the production of endurance, character and hope and in the experience of God's love.[44] The brand-marks received in the service of Jesus are clearly a source of pride and joy to the apostle,[45] and the thorn in the flesh proves to be a means of grace.[46]

(iii) Peace

The theme of peace runs constantly through the Bible. In the sense of an 'end to hostilities', this is not to be wondered at, for Israel, small as she was in geographical size, was the envy of the surrounding nations and, consequently, the target of their desires. She was pounced upon and invaded, her cities raided, her inhabitants deported. Sometimes she won, and the enemy withdrew. Then it was that "the land had rest, peace," for a period of years – the phrase is almost a refrain in some of the nation's story-books.

With the passing of time, the word took on a more profound meaning. Used of the nation, it stood for that nation's well-being in every facet of its life. It described a community which enjoyed God's blessing, his protection and favour, his gentle grace. The prophets saw peace as a by-product, it was the fruit of a nation's rightness with its God. "The wicked are like a troubled sea, a sea that cannot rest, whose troubled waters cast up mud and filth. There is no peace for the wicked, says the Lord."[47] The prophets never tired of asserting that if social conditions were unjust, if there was neglect of the widow and denial of a proper wage to the worker, if the poor were down-trodden and immorality abounded, if relationships of one group with another were broken and *therefore* relationship with God was impaired, then there could be no community, no communion, no peace.[48] There is a national connotation to 'peace' which is of fundamental importance. It is more than the mere cessation of hostilities. It is 'salvation' seen in its outcome. It is life lived in its freedom and fullness.

When we turn to the New Testament, the word takes on an even deeper and more personal meaning. We watch Jesus at work and we see individuals not only forsaking relationships inimical to their peace but also entering into a fullness of life which hitherto they had not been able to experience. The woman who had interrupted the Pharisee's meal and had lavished her devotion on Jesus leaves the meal forgiven and "goes into peace".[49] The demon-possessed man, a terror to himself and a menace to the community, meets Christ and is found "sitting at his feet clothed and in his right mind".[50] The little civil servant Zacchaeus, whose relationships had gone awry, finds that, in his contact with the Rabbi from the north, "salvation has come to his house".[51] He was now enabled to live in joy and wellbeing, at peace with God, with his neighbours and with himself.

In the writings of Paul, peace is a dominant theme. "The kingdom of God is not eating and drinking, but justice, *peace*, and joy inspired by the Holy Spirit."[52] The old middle-wall which separated Jew from Gentile has, in Christ, been broken down and the two are made one – a single new humanity being created in him. Here is a humanity without barriers; peace has been made.[53] And there is peace for the individual – "now that we have been justified through faith, we have peace with God through our Lord Jesus Christ, through whom we have been allowed to enter the sphere of God's grace, where we now stand."[54] Peace *with* God having thus been achieved, we are now able to enjoy the peace *of* God, which is beyond our utmost understanding and which "will keep guard" over our hearts and our thoughts in Christ Jesus.[55]

Here, then, in 'peace with God' and in 'the peace of God', we see the normal state of man as God purposed it to be – his intention fulfilled for the universe, the nation, the individual.

When Paul prayed for the Church at Rome, "may the God of hope fill you with all joy and peace by your faith in him", he prayed for a church as God destined it to be, free, unfettered, abounding in life. And that applies to the individual too – in this life and the next. For Elizabeth Goudge was right when she wrote: "I believe that death interrupts nothing of importance if the goal is Christ."[56]

(iv) Longsuffering (AV; *patience*, RSV and NEB)

In his great hymn to love, Paul says: "Love is patient".[57] Here in Galatians 5: 22 love and patience are linked again as first and fourth in the list. Patience is an outcome of love.

Perhaps the best approach to an understanding of the ethical quality of patience is to view it as a reflection of the patience of God (an aspect of his character to which too little attention has been given). Teilhard de Chardin, life-long worker in the field of palaeo-anthropology, saw it as his mission to interpret the Christian faith in terms which would not do despite to the thinking and concepts of scientists, philosophers and theologians. He was an intrepid visionary of cosmo-genesis, the movement of the universe to its evolutionary goal. He helped us to think of God as the God of the galaxies. In his *Hymn of the Universe* he has this remarkable passage:

The prodigious expanses of time which preceded the first Christmas were not empty of Christ: they were imbued with the influx of his power. It was the ferment of his conception that stirred up the cosmic masses and directed the initial developments of the biosphere. It was the travail preceding his birth that accelerated the development of instinct and the birth of thought upon the earth. Let us have done with the stupidity which makes a stumbling-block of the endless eras of expectancy imposed on us by the Messiah; the fearful, anonymous labours of primitive man, the beauty fashioned through the age-long history of ancient Egypt, the anxious expectancy of Israel, the patient distilling of the attar of oriental mysticism, the endless refining of wisdom by the Greeks: all these were needed before the Flower could blossom on the rod of Jesse and of all humanity. All these preparatory processes were cosmologically and biologically necessary that Christ might set foot upon our human stage.[58]

Teilhard de Chardin's God was the God of long patience – "Source, Guide and Goal of all that is", as Paul puts it.[59] "Let us return to Paul," de Chardin exclaimed in his *Essai d'intégration de l'homme dans l'univers*. "It was", says his biographer, "a journey that he could not take too often."[60] His mind found a congenial partner in the writer of such Christological passages as Ephesians 1: 10, where Paul speaks of God's purpose being to bring the universe, all in heaven and earth, into a unity in Christ, and Colossians 1: 13–20, where again, the whole universe having been created through Christ and for Christ, the reconciliation of all things, whether on earth or in heaven, is envisaged through him alone.

Within a more restricted frame of reference, the patience and longsuffering of God can be traced in the history of Israel. Paul refers specifically to this in the shocked question which he puts to the Romans: "Do you think lightly of his wealth of kindness, of tolerance, and of *patience*, without recognising that God's kindness is meant to lead you to a change of heart?"[61] That patience had been sorely tested by a nation which had gone "a-whoring" after false gods and which had interpreted its election in terms of privilege rather than of responsibility and missionary service. For all its refractoriness and pride, a remnant remained through whom God's purpose and patience might be made plain for all to see. God's patient toleration led to his making "known the full wealth of his splendour . . ."[62]

We have thought of God's patience displayed in the long evolution of the universe, and in the history of Israel. But what of his patience with individuals? There is a remarkable passage in the first Epistle to Timothy in which the writer, reflecting on the days when he had met Christ "with abuse and persecution and outrage", now sees himself as a kind of specimen – dare we say a show-piece? – a "first occasion for displaying all his patience", for all men to see. The first among sinners, the erstwhile persecutor of the Church is now Christ's servant and apostle. No wonder that the passage ends with the doxology: "Now to the King of all worlds, immortal, invisible, the only God, be honour and glory for ever and ever!"[63]

T. Olivers (1725–99) catches something of the awesomeness of God's eternity and patience in the words:

> The God who reigns on high
> The great Archangels sing,
> And "Holy, Holy, Holy" cry,
> "Almighty King!
> Who was, and is, the same,
> And evermore shall be;
> Eternal Father, great I AM,
> We worship Thee."

Paul, in including patience in his list, hints that this aspect of the God of the galaxies, the God of history, the God of individual grace, should in some tiny measure be reflected in the character of his children. The reverse is often the case. Impatience expressing itself in irritability; the emphasis on speed rather than on quality; irritation with *ourselves* because our spiritual growth is so slow – these are manifestations of the opposite of that patience which is the outcome of love. We do well to remind ourselves that the *essential* things, like the growth of a foetus in the womb or the growth of wheat in a field, cannot (at least without detriment) be hurried. They are instances of nature's patience. That is how the real work is done, and the real world sustained.[64]

The remaining five items in the list in Galatians 5: 22–3 can be dealt with more summarily. We may take 'kindness' and 'goodness' together. The meaning of one flows over into the other.

(v) Kindness (NEB and RSV; *gentleness*, AV) and *(vi) goodness* (NEB, RSV and AV)

Both derive from the essential character of God who alone is wholly kind and fully good. In so far as these qualities are manifested in the Christian, they are due to the operation of God in his heart. God's "kindness to us in Christ Jesus", once received, overflows in kindness to others, for, as Paul says in this same letter, "where light is, there all goodness springs up, all justice and truth".[65] God's gracious attitude and acts towards sinners are reflected in a like attitude on the part of the redeemed sinner towards others. Our "patience and kindliness",[66] marks by which we are "recommended" to others, are the fruit of the Spirit within us. Harriet Auber was correct when she wrote:

> And every virtue we possess,
> And every victory won,
> And every thought of holiness,
> *Are his alone.*

"What room then is left for human pride? It is excluded."[67]

(vii) Faith (AV; *fidelity*, NEB; *faithfulness*, RV and RSV)

Paul uses this word *(pistis)* in three ways, and it is important to distinguish them.

The *least* frequent meaning is "the Faith", the Christian message. "The faith which once he tried to destroy" is a case in point;[68] and many take the occurrence of the word in Galatians 3: 23 and 25 ("before the Christian message came"; "now that the Christian message has come") in a similar sense.

The *most* frequent meaning of the word in the writings of Paul is that of transference of trust from self to God or, as Bornkamm puts it, "acceptance, in obedient trust and trustful obedience, of God's saving act as proclaimed in the gospel".[69] Such passages of auto-biography as Galatians 1: 13 ff. and Philippians 3: 4 ff. illustrate what faith in this sense meant to the apostle in his relationship with God.[70]

There is a third meaning of the word, comparatively less frequent but of importance from an ethical point of view. In this sense it means faithfulness, fidelity, trust-worthiness, reliability. It is in this sense that Paul uses the word here.

Just as we have seen that the best approach to an understanding of the ethical quality of patience was to view it as a reflection of the patience of God, so the quality of faithfulness is best seen as a reflection of the total reliability of God himself. The God of Old Testa-ment and New Testament is a *covenant* God. He takes the initiative in entering into a covenant relationship with his people (through Abraham, Noah, Moses, David, and so on). Having done so, whatever the re-sponse of his people may be, he himself can be trusted to keep faith. He is the *Amen*, the utterly reliable God who does not go back on his word. The ethical quality of faithfulness may be a very down-to-earth one, but its source is in heaven.

What it means with regard to faithfulness to our marriage promises;[71] to our business and financial con-tracts (our word, our bond); to our keeping of appoint-ments; to our confirmation or ordination vows – all these matters, and many besides, are directly related to this aspect of the fruit of the Spirit, and must constantly be reviewed in the light of the God who himself is the supremely faithful One.

There is a hint of steel in this concept of faithfulness and fidelity. It is a close cousin of that word which is a favourite of the New Testament writers (though it does not occur in the list in Galatians 5) and which is gener-ally translated 'patience' in the Authorised Version. The translation is weak. 'Steady endurance' or 'forti-tude' is nearer the mark. Paul regards it as a character-istic of God himself – he is "the source of all *fortitude* and all encouragement";[72] and of Christ himself – he had often heard from the early Christians of "the *steadfastness* of Christ" which marked his ministry.[73] "If we endure," – it is the verb from which the noun 'fortitude' is derived – "we shall reign with him"; the words of this ancient hymn have an eschatological connotation.[74]

There is nothing dour about this concept nor about its cousin 'faithfulness'. It is not a stark, barren, negative quality. It has a glow about it because it looks toward a goal. For it was said of Jesus that, "for the joy that was set before him, he endured the cross, making light of the shame".[75] That was faithfulness to the end.

Let two modern writers, John Buchan and Elizabeth Goudge, add their comments:

> I reckon fortitude's the biggest thing a man can have – just to go on enduring when there's no guts or heart left in you . . . But the head man at the job was the Apostle Paul . . .[76]

> To love God subtly alters a human being. If the simile is not too homely, the lover of God has glue in his veins and tends to be more adherent than other men. The more he loves God the more, for God's sake, he sticks to his woman, his job or his faith. Christians should be judged, I think, by their stickableness, since by that alone can God get anything done in this world.[77]

(viii) Gentleness (NEB and RSV; *meekness* AV)
This word occurs again, in the company of another word variously translated as 'gentleness' or 'magnanimity', in a description of the character of Christ.[78] Here is a picture of very great value, derived either from Paul's actual meeting with the Lord in the flesh or from the detailed impressions of him which early disciples had gained and shared with the apostle. Gentleness and magnanimity were the marks of Christ – gentleness

which had about it no suggestion of weakness but rather of the strength of love. ('Meekness' today too often has about it an element of weakness which it originally lacked.) These qualities manifested themselves in the everyday life and conduct of Christ, and were shown in the fullness of their glory on the cross where, with a saving gentleness, "he humbled himself, and in obedience accepted even death".[79]

This word 'gentleness' meets us again in Galatians 6: 1. Here a situation is envisaged in which someone, on a sudden impulse, has done something wrong. It is then for the Christian brothers to "set him right again *very gently*" – with no arrogance, no impatience, only with the gentle strength of love.

(ix) Self-control (NEB and RSV; temperance, AV)

The Authorised Version translation 'temperance' clearly will not do, for in our modern use of the word it is too often associated with abstinence from drink. The word has a much wider reference than that. It is frequently used with the idea of sexual restraint as, for example, in the sentence: "If they cannot control themselves, they should marry."[80] Indeed, the occurrence of the word in the list we are considering suggests a contrast particularly with those marks of "the lower nature; fornication, impurity, and indecency" which Paul had just mentioned.

But the word by itself means simply self-control, and it takes its particular meaning from the context in which it occurs. Thus, in a famous passage where Paul uses the illustration of athletics, he says that every athlete exercises self-control – presumably in matters of diet, hours of sleep, and so on; the free translation of the New English Bible is "goes into strict training".[81] And the *general* meaning of 'self-control' appears again when Paul before Felix turns "to questions of morals, *self-control*, and the coming judgement".[82]

Here in the list of Galatians 5: 23, this self-control is

seen as Christ-control, for it is a fruit of his Spirit. This divine mastery leads to perfect freedom – "to serve him is to reign". George Matheson put it well in the hymn which begins:

> Make me a captive, Lord,
> And then I shall be free.

We have spent some care on considering the "harvest of the Spirit", for in the nine words which we have been studying we have an outline of Paul's ethical teaching and, doubtless, a description of what it meant to him to be a liberated man in Christ. Like any other Christian, he had his ups and downs, but God was at work in him; and things belonging to the Spirit were living and growing in him, and he was being "shaped to the likeness of God's Son". And God saw what he was making, and it was good.

But now we have a very considerable problem to face. So far we have been moving in the realm of personal freedom, of individual ethics, of the growth of Christian character. But Paul also moved in the first century, as we do in the twentieth, in a wider world where things had gone grievously wrong, where might prevailed over right, where the groans of the oppressed could be heard on every hand. Indeed, Paul refers to this *in general* when he writes of the created universe as being "the victim of frustration", groaning "in all its parts as if in the pangs of childbirth".[83] When we come to examine his letters, we are bound to be struck by a lack of denunciation of some current evils which, to say the least, is surprising. The prophets of the Old Testament were not slow to inveigh against current wrongs in society and to do so in specific and pointed terms. Note how Amos denounces the exploitation of the poor: "Listen to this, you cows of Bashan . . . you who oppress the poor and crush the destitute, who say to your lords, 'Bring us drink': the Lord God has sworn by his holiness that your time is coming when men shall carry you away . . . You shall each be carried straight out through the breaches in the walls and pitched on a dung hill."[84] Isaiah, too, depicts the Lord opening "the indictment against the elders of his people . . . You have ravaged the vineyard, and the spoils of the poor are in your houses. Is it nothing to you that you crush my people and grind the faces of the poor?"[85] Instances could be multiplied again and again. Jesus himself, in such parables as those of the Good Samaritan and the Sheep and the Goats,[86] is in line with the great Hebrew prophetic tradition, and so is such a New Testament writer as James: "Weep and wail over the miserable fate descending on you," he writes to people who had great possessions.[87] Paul is indeed vividly aware of the wrath of God "revealed from heaven and falling upon all the godless wickedness of men".[88] That provides a sombre background to his thinking. But it is when we come to look for a more specific denunciation of current iniquities and inequities that we find ourselves surprised by its absence. For instance, slavery and the position of women in the first-century world were issues which cried out for protest. What do we find that Paul did in relation to them? Let us examine the matter.

(i) Slavery
Of the extent of this feature of life in the world of Paul's day there can be no doubt. Writing of the period of Augustus – he died when Paul was a boy – John Buchan refers to slavery as "that canker of the old world". He goes on:

The wars of Rome during her great period of expansion had filled the city and the country districts with slaves, most of them from races of a high civilisation. In a rich family there were men and women skilled in every task from the most menial to the most expert. There was no need for a Roman to go outside his household for any craftsman. Slaves were secretaries,

155

copyists and accountants; carpenters, metal-workers, jewellers, weavers and plumbers; cooks, bakers, and coiffeurs; managers of country estates as well as rural labourers; painters, artists, and builders; physicians, surgeons and oculists. Their economic value put a certain bridle upon a master's caprice, but their position was always precarious. They could be flogged or branded at their master's will, in a criminal trial their evidence was given under torture, and strict limits were set to their acquisition of property. It was the fashion to expose a sick slave in the temple of Aesculapius on an island in the Tiber, and leave his recovery to chance.[89]

No doubt, many masters were humane, and there must have been a certain number of slaves who were like the Hebrew ones of an earlier day who preferred to remain as they were – "I love my master, . . . I will not go free".[90] But for every one who was fortunate enough to be in this position, there must have been thousands who groaned under their master's yoke, resenting bitterly their status in a society which regarded them as no better than chattels. Their dignity as human beings was affronted when they were lined up on the quay-side and prodded like so many cattle ready for sale to the highest bidder. What this must have entailed in the break-up of families and of hearts can scarcely be imagined.

What did Paul do about this? He seems to have been content almost to take the status quo for granted. Thus he could write to the Colossians: "Slaves, give entire obedience to your earthly masters, not merely with an outward show of service, to curry favour with men, but with single-mindedness, out of reverence for the Lord. Whatever you are doing, put your whole heart into it, as if you were doing it for the Lord and not for men, knowing that there is a Master who will give you your heritage as a reward for your service. Christ is the Master whose slaves you must be. Dishonesty will be requited, and he has no favourites."[91] True, this is followed by a brief injunction to the masters – "be just and fair to your slaves, knowing that you too have a Master in heaven." There is a similar passage in the letter to the Ephesians, where the injunction to the masters is elaborated.[92] There is an element in such passages which has provided the excuse in later centuries for a *laissez-faire* attitude to social injustice. (We may compare the instruction given by John the Baptist to the soldiers – "make do with your pay!")[93] "Pie in the sky when you die" is little comfort when *upstairs* there is luxury and even cruelty, and *downstairs* there is oppression and poor wages.

Have we touched here on a blind spot in the apostle? There are matters to be considered on the other side. *First*, Paul was a man whose mission was almost blindingly clear. He was not, in any primary sense, sent on an errand of social amelioration. He was sent to plant the Church in the main centres of the Roman world, to tend its growth, to turn men from darkness to light and from the power of Satan to God, and, that having been done, to outline certain basic ethical principles (such as we have studied in Galatians 5: 22–3), which the members of the churches must work out in the rough and tumble of everyday life. He was an evangelist and only in a derivative and secondary sense a social reformer.

Secondly, Paul was a strategist. "There is a time for silence and a time for speech", as the wise man said.[94] Consider what would have happened had Paul embarked on a campaign for the abolition of slavery or even of its worst features. The result would almost certainly have been his own arrest – he would not have minded that very much – and also the silencing of his message and the premature ending of his journeys. So ingrained a part of first-century society was slavery that protest, *at that point in history*, might well have been worse than useless. It might well have been counter-productive to his whole mission. He had enough on his hands without undertaking the impossible effort of effecting the political change involved in the abolition of slavery.

This being the case, what was he to do? He was a man of compassion, and often his heart must have been deeply grieved at what he saw in the treatment of slaves by their owners. He was not wholly helpless. There were at least two courses of action open to him, the first small in scale but with great possibilities in it, the second more basic and limitless in its outworkings.

First, in his own contacts with slaves, he could show something of the compassion of Christ and the dignity of the slave concerned which would undoubtedly be observed by others. We have an outstanding instance of this reflected in the most 'gentlemanly' of his letters, the Epistle to Philemon. It is entirely concerned with the welfare of a runaway slave, Onesimus, whose spiritual father Paul had become when they were fellow-prisoners. It is not hard to re-construct the situation: Paul leading the slave to know him whose service is perfect freedom; the slave gratefully caring for the needs of the older man, his fellow-slave of Jesus Christ. Paul would have liked to keep him, for he had become "*a dear brother* . . . both as man and as Christian"[95] and (with a nice pun on the meaning of the name Onesimus) very *useful* to him. But that would not do. He must go back to the master to whom he belonged. Philemon was asked to receive him back – "a part of myself" – and to welcome him "as you would welcome me". The plea was surely irresistible. Paul assumed that Onesimus' status as a slave would continue. He did not ask his master to free him. But he did ask that there should be such a relationship between the two men that they would see themselves to be brothers in the Lord.

It was a charming letter. But it was much more. For it established the essential dignity and worth of Onesimus and, in doing so, left Philemon in no doubt as to how he should treat him.

All of which leads to the *second* course of action open to Paul, a course of action which I have called basic and limitless in its outworkings. Paul was a theologian. He was concerned with the basics of theology and of life. The whole structure of slavery will be undermined, once masters begin to understand the doctrine of the *Abba*-God, the meaning of the grace of our Lord Jesus Christ, and the significance of the Church at whose central service masters and slaves kneel side by side on level ground. There is life in this doctrine so powerful that it can be compared to that of the tiny acorn which, given time to grow and put forth its innate strength, has power to undermine a building's foundations.

> The silent activity
> of yeast
> in dough;
> doubling, trebling, its size,
> transforming
> its substance.
>
> The delicate searching thrust
> of blades of grass
> through the dark soil;
> invisibly
> clothing
> the bare earth
> in green.
>
> The persistent pressure
> of brittle roots
> against stone,
> until the crack is seen.
>
> A man,
> vulnerable,
> crucified,
> imprisoned in a tomb,
> yet breaking through
> the stubborn rock
> which cannot hold
> God's love.[96]

God's truth is like that. God's truth about the nature of man, as revealed to Paul, and hence about our attitude to slavery is like that. Its outworkings are incalculable. Paul knew what he was doing. Perhaps instead of blaming him for not leading an anti-slavery campaign, we should marvel at the slowness of the Church in ensuing years in not working out the implications of Christian doctrine. Society should not have been compelled to wait for a Wesley or a Shaftesbury before the wickedness of this evil was exposed in the light of the Gospel, for all to see. The seeds of Liberation Theology at its best are within Paul's letters.

"Gone is the distinction between ... slave and freeman."[97] Factually in Christ, yes. Actually in society – how long, O Lord, how long?

(ii) The position of women

"There has probably seldom been anyone at the same time hated with such fiery hatred and loved with such strong passion as Paul" – so wrote Adolf Deissmann.[98] One of the reasons for his being "hated with such fiery hatred" has been his attitude to women and to sex, as people have understood that attitude – or misunderstood it. "St Paul has always interested me, though I never liked him, perhaps because I believe that he had little use for women!" – so wrote a highly intelligent recent correspondent, herself a woman. "In regard to the status of women in social or domestic life Paul's mind appears to have been in a state of arrested development ... Paul had not been able to shake himself free from Jewish theory and the Rabbinic arguments by which it was supported" – so wrote no less a scholar than Anderson Scott.[99]

The matter is not a simple one. It deserves some careful examination. And first – for the minor question has some bearing on the major one – was Paul married? No firm answer can be given, but there is much to be said for thinking that he was. Marriage and the begetting of children was to the Jew a sacred duty. Had not the Creator said, "Be fruitful and multiply"? According to the Talmudic rule, a young Jew should marry at the age of eighteen. Rabbi Eliezer (admittedly writing about the year AD 90 but enunciating a principle going back many years) wrote: "He who does not engage in propagation of the race is as though he shed blood."[100] There is another saying: "God waits until a man is twenty; but if a man is not married by his twentieth year, then God says, may his spirit vanish." Of course, Paul may have been the exception. He may have been the odd man out. But the burden of probability is against this. It is likely that he married. There are, indeed, those who think that the way he writes about married life in 1 Corinthians 7 indicates that he knows it from the inside, but I am not sure that a great deal of weight can be put on this argument. It is possible that his wife was an unbeliever and that, on this score, they parted – "if . . . the heathen partner wishes for a separation, let him have it."[101] When he spoke of suffering the loss of all things for the sake of Christ[102] this loss may have included the consolations of a wife and home; certainly anyone married to a man engaged on such journeys as Paul undertook would have seen very little of him! Perhaps the question, "Was Paul married?" can best be answered: "We do not know, but it is likely that he was."

His attitude to marriage was coloured by his belief in the imminent return of the Lord – "the time we live in will not last long" – a belief which proved to be mistaken. But it was also coloured by his concern that nothing, no other care or anxiety, should detract from a Christian's devotion to the cause of Christ:[103] and here he may well have been speaking from the background of his own experience.

We turn now to the larger matter of his attitude to women. Paul was no woman-hater – we have only to read Romans 16 to see with what affection and respect he greeted them (and, in passing, we note that in v. 7 the second name may equally well be the feminine Junia, and so we get a glimpse of husband and wife working together "among the apostles"). What he did hate was the degradation of women – and this he found in abundance in the heathen cities to which he travelled. The sex-cults of the ancient world flourished and abounded.

The passage in 1 Corinthians 11: 2–16, about a woman having her head covered has been widely misunderstood. So far from this passage being a reflection on the dignity or status of a woman, it would seem rather to be designed to protect her. It is hard for us in the West, living in an era of emancipation for women, to put ourselves back into the setting of the first century. Perhaps Sir William Ramsay will help us as well as anyone to get this right:

> In Oriental lands the veil is the power and the honour and the dignity of the woman. With the veil on her head, she can go anywhere in security and profound respect. She is not seen; it is the mark of thoroughly bad manners to observe a veiled woman in the streets. She is alone. The rest of the people around are non-existent to her, as she is to them. She is supreme in the crowd. She passes at her own free choice, and a space must be left for her. The man who did anything to annoy or molest her would have a bad time in an Oriental town and might easily lose his life. A man's house is his castle, in so far as a lady is understood to be there; without her it is free to any stranger to enter as guest or temporary lord.
>
> But without the veil the woman is a thing of nought, whom any one may insult. The true Oriental, if uneducated in Western ways, seems to be inclined naturally to treat with rudeness, to push and ill-treat a European lady in the street. A woman's authority and dignity vanish along with the all-covering veil that she discards. That is the Oriental view which Paul learned in Tarsus.[104]

This was no trivial matter. The enactment to wear veils, possibly made by Paul at their request, marked the Christian woman off clearly from the woman of the heathen temples, whose sexuality was degraded in the name of their religious cults.

What are we to say about the passage in which Paul lays it down that "women should not address the meeting. They have no licence to speak, but should keep their place as the law directs. If there is something they want to know, they can ask their husbands at home. It is a shocking thing that a woman should address the congregation."[105] If this passage is genuine, it may well be that, once again, Paul was laying down the injunction in order to protect the women concerned, in a society which might well have interpreted such 'liberty' as a sign of moral laxity. But there are serious difficulties in accepting the Pauline authorship of these verses – they are interruptive of the argument; in some manuscripts they come after verse 40, and this points to a later interpolation; and so on. But the greatest difficulty in accepting them is that they appear to contradict an earlier passage in this same Epistle where Paul took it for granted that women prayed and prophesied in public.[106] More importantly, they seem to deny that position which he adopted elsewhere when he accepted and welcomed the service of women as fellow-workers in the Gospel. If Paul was consistent – and consistency does not appear to be his greatest virtue! – then we may doubt the authenticity of verses 34–5, *or* we may take them as a further attempt on Paul's part to protect women from that degradation of their sexuality which was more rampant in Corinth than perhaps anywhere else in the contemporary world.

When we are considering such matters as the veiling of a woman's head and her silence before a congregation, we may note the words with which Gillian Clark concludes her article on "The Women at Corinth": "We need not let first-century anxieties restrict the twentieth-century use of women in ministry: they had different problems at Corinth."[107]

In a frank criticism of the Declaration of the Congregation for the Doctrine of the Faith that "Jesus intended in principle to exclude women from the priestly ministry for all times and under all sociological conditions", Karl Rahner argues thus:

> . . . we can say confidently and with adequately certain historical knowledge that in the cultural and sociological situation at the time Jesus and the early Church could not in practice have considered and still less set up any female congregational leaders or presidents of the eucharistic celebration . . . any more than Jesus or Paul could have been expected to notice explicitly the contradiction between their fundamental appreciation of human dignity and the acceptance of slavery as it existed at the time and still less to attempt expressly to oppose and to abolish this slavery.[108]

This is a weighty judgement on both the issues – slavery, and the position of women – which we are considering.

The true charter for women, so far as Paul is concerned, is the same as that which he established for slaves: "There is no such thing as Jew and Greek, slave and freeman, *male and female*; for you are all one person in Christ Jesus".[109] There were three great divides in the ancient world – race (Jew and Greek), class (slave and freeman), and sex (male and female). (Who is to say that they are not still the three great divides of the modern world?) But when men and women come to be "in Christ", then they become members of that new humanity in which the old distinctions, the ancient divisions, count no more. No wonder that E. F. Scott once wrote that Paul "was one of the great pioneers in the emancipation of women".[110] How could it be otherwise? Men and women alike have the same value in the sight of God; they are on an equal footing before him.

Anyone who could write about the marriage-relationship of husband and wife in the terms in which the author of Ephesians 5: 25 ff. wrote can never be described as a disparager of women. "Husbands, love your wives, as Christ also loved the church and gave himself up for it . . ." Such was the love of Christ for the Church that he was willing to die for it. Such should be the love of husband for wife. One cannot go further than that. Those who make most of the 'subjection' of wives to husbands – and this is an authentic note in the letter to the Ephesians[111] – must mark well that it is written in the context of a passage in which *mutual* submission is enjoined. Perhaps 'defer' would not be far from a true translation – "defer to one another", husband to wife and wife to husband. "Perhaps it is not really difficult to see what St Paul means", writes Lindsay Dewar; "he means, 'try to put yourself in the position of the other person and so learn to appreciate his point of view' . . . In fact, St Paul is really only saying in another way, 'Show *agape* towards'; for the essence of *agape* consists in putting oneself, or trying to put oneself, in the other person's place."[112]

Nor need we be nervous about the implication of those passages where Paul speaks of the 'headship' of the man in relation to the woman. "The head preserves the body from harm. The brain controls the limbs and saves them from accidents. So too the Head of the Church saves his members from destruction and from the disintegration which sin would cause apart from his saving grace."[113] There is no fear in such love. There need be no fear in taking such an analogy seriously.

As in the matter of slavery, so in the matter of the position of women in society, the acorn of Pauline doctrine waited long for germination and growth. Even yet its eruptive power has not been fully felt. Until it is, society, and the Church within society, will be enfeebled by inequalities which give rise to bitterness and frustration, and by a ministry impoverished because of its one-sided masculinity. We repeat: "Gone is the distinction between . . . male and female." Factually in

Christ, yes. Actually in society – how long, O Lord, how long?

The ethics of Paul, we saw at the beginning of this chapter, are the ethics of a liberated man. They have proved to be the means of liberation for great numbers in every generation of the Church's history. But to how many millions of others in days gone by – and today – they have failed to bring freedom because it has proved easier to evade the implications, individual and communal, which these ethics carry with them! A measure of daring – shall we say of heroism? – is called for in following the lead of the apostle; abandonment of safety was the price he paid in following his Lord.

CHURCHMAN

The mystical body of thy Son, which is the blessed
company of all faithful people.
Book of Common Prayer (post-Communion collect)

> In the communion of thy saints,
> Is wisdom, safety, and delight;
> And when my heart declines and faints,
> It's raisèd by their heat and light.
>
> As for my friends, they are not lost;
> The several vessels of thy fleet,
> Though parted now, by tempests tossed,
> Shall safely in the haven meet.
> Richard Baxter

Certain it is that for St Paul . . . to be a Christian is to be
a member of a living organism whose life derives from
Christ. There is no other way of being a Christian. In
this sense, Christian experience is always ecclesiastical
experience.

J. S. Whale: *Christian Doctrine*

CHURCHMAN

To belong to the people of God, to be a member of the assembly of the Lord's faithful ones, had been an integral part of the religion of Saul of Tarsus from his earliest days. "Circumcised on my eighth day, Israelite by race, of the tribe of Benjamin, a Hebrew born and bred."[1] No one with a background such as that could sit loose to the privileges and responsibilities of community membership. He could not have any truck with a religion which put individualism, however pious, above the privilege of belonging to the divinely chosen *ekklesia* – the word is frequently used in the Old Testament of that community which was no casual aggregation of like-minded people, but was indeed the solemn assembly of the people of God. There was something very special about a community which included among its regulations such an injunction as this: "No descendant of an irregular union, even down to the tenth generation, shall become a member of the assembly of the Lord."[2] "The members of this community were *hagioi*, 'holy', 'consecrated' like the 'saints of the Most High', whose kingdom was, in Daniel 7: 9–28, the manifestation of the Son of Man."[3]

Paul's visits to the Temple in Jerusalem must have impressed on his young mind how magnificent a thing it was to belong to a people such as this, whose focus of worship found so superb a centre. "Look, Master, what huge stones! What fine buildings!" – he could well have echoed the words which the disciples addressed to Jesus with such pride.[4] As he surveyed, and took part in, the Temple worship, he must often have looked round on his fellow-Jews and murmured: "They are Israelites . . .

theirs is the splendour of the divine presence, theirs the covenants, the law, the temple worship, and the promises."[5] It was all a very precious heritage.

As for the synagogues – those local manifestations of Jewish piety, education and law – he had been familiar with them from his youngest days. There he had learnt to pray. There he had become a man of the Book – his roots went down deep into Scripture. There he watched Gentiles 'listening in' to what Judaism had to say about God and man and the ethics of community living. There he saw increasing numbers of them being drawn towards the monotheistic faith of his people. He was proud to belong to a race which could give such a faith to the world. To be a churchman – we here use the word in its Old Testament sense – was precious indeed.

All this was an essential ingredient in the make-up of the man who met Christ on the Damascus road. But at that point a radical change took place in his thinking.

The basic change in Paul when he became a Christian seems to have been in the understanding of what constituted membership in God's people. For the Jews of his day (and ever since, I take it), the most important of all blessings is to be within the Covenant. Born into Judaism, circumcised, and observant of the Jewish way of life, a Jew is assumed to be within the Covenant – he belongs, he is at home, he is safe; and if he is to be put outside, he has deliberately to flout the Law, deliberately to excommunicate himself. The Jew is in the Ark unless he deliberately throws himself overboard. But of non-Jews no such assumption is made . . . There is a privilege that belongs to Judaism and does not extend its borders – the privilege of being within the Covenant.

Now, it is this, I believe, that, for Paul, the encounter with Jesus radically changed. He comes (ultimately, at least) to a new understanding of membership of God's people. What he found in Jesus was shattering to his previous position. In Jesus of

Nazareth he found one who had incurred the worst possible ostracism from Israel . . . Yet this Jesus now turned out to be the epitome of Israel. The Jesus whom Paul encountered was divinely vindicated, exalted in glory, and accepted by God as his Chosen One, the embodiment of all that Israel was intended to be. Such was the one who had gone through the most ignominious death and had been formally rejected by the highest religious authorities. Israel's exile is Israel's first citizen – and more. This meant . . . that God's Chosen One is not one who is segregated and kept safe, but one who suffers the worst that man can suffer. And that, in its turn, meant that *Israel could not cherish a spiritual élitism any longer.*[6]

Certain Old Testament concepts about the people of God had therefore to be radically reviewed, revised, and enlarged, when Paul the Jew became Paul the apostolic Christian. Not least was this so in his thinking about Israel as the Bride of Christ.

The idea, with all its suggestions of tender and loving intimacy, was one which the prophets frequently developed. But the development was often in a minor key, for Israel had so often been unfaithful and had gone "a-whoring" after other gods, the Chosen People faithless to the Choosing God. The great eighth-century prophet Hosea illustrated the theme from his own experience of domestic tragedy, his wife Gomer having proved unfaithful to him in spite of all his unfailing love for her. So, he saw, it was with Israel and her God, her divine husband. And if exile must necessarily be the consequence of such "adultery", even there God would be with her. "But now listen, I will woo her, I will go with her into the wilderness and comfort her: there I will restore her vineyards, turning the Vale of Trouble into the Gate of Hope, and there she will answer as in her youth, when she came up out of Egypt. On that day she will call me 'My husband' and shall no more call me 'My Baal'; for I will wipe from her lips the very names of the Baalim; never again shall their names be heard. This is the very word of the Lord."[7] It is hard to conceive of a passage more tender than this.

Jeremiah echoed the theme: "Do you see what apostate Israel did? She went up to every hill-top and under every spreading tree, and there she played the whore. Even after she had done all this, I said to her, 'Come back to me', but she would not."[8] So did Ezekiel in his detailed and moving parable of the foundling.[9]

But the same imagery of bride and bridegroom was developed in a major key of great rejoicing, especially by the prophet of the exile in such passages as Isaiah 61: 10, and 62: 4–5; we need quote only one verse: "As a young man weds a maiden, so you shall wed him who rebuilds you, and your God shall rejoice over you as a bridegroom rejoices over the bride."[10]

All this wealth of imagery, then, was to hand for Paul to use. But first he had to be clear as to what constituted the Israel of God. He pondered this in the light of what he was learning of the love of God as shown in the Person of Christ. It became clear to him that God's forgiving grace was poured out on men and women quite irrespective of the race to which they belonged. God had no favourites – Jew and Gentile were equally precious to him. If this was so – and he could not deny it as he went on his travels among the new little churches of God's people – the great Lover, the heavenly bridegroom, had a new Israel as his bride, an Israel composed of all those, of all races, on whose "lips is the confession 'Jesus is Lord', and in whose heart the faith that God raised him from the dead".[11] The bride of the Lord took on a meaning and a magnificence which the prophets had only adumbrated.

At this point Paul, naturally enough, joined his thinking about the Church as the *Bride* of Christ with his thinking about the Church as the *Body* of Christ. In marriage, the two, the man and the woman, become one flesh. In the marriage of Christ and his Church, they are one Body. "For just as in a single human body there are many limbs and organs, all with different functions, so all of us, united with Christ, form one body, serving individually as limbs and organs to one another."[12] Paul got a vision of "one body and one Spirit".[13] He made the clear identification – "his body which is the church".[14] The great similes of Bride and Body coalesce, and are elaborated with considerable detail in the classic passage in Ephesians 5: 22–3.[15]

It seems likely that Paul's radical re-thinking of the imagery of the Bride began – or, at least, took a dramatic step forward – at the point when he met the Lord on the Damascus road. For the question addressed to him, which must have smitten him with immense force, was *not* "Saul, Saul, why do you persecute my Church?", but "Saul, Saul, why do you persecute *me*?" (The point is made, in identical words, in all three accounts of his conversion in Acts.) Christ and his Christians were *one*. Touch them, and you touch him. Injure them, and you injure him. Persecute them, and you persecute him. They are his body.

It would seem highly likely, too, that, on their missionary journeys together, "dear doctor Luke" would have explained more fully to the apostle the closeness of connection, the inter-relatedness, of head to body and of limb to limb. "If one member suffers, all the members suffer with it." We can hear the voice of Luke chiming in with Paul's in the passages in his letters which deal with this theme.[16]

This inter-relatedness is developed by Paul in a third metaphor, that of the *building*, the rising Temple whose foundation is Christ and whose strong growth, like the development of a healthy body, depends on the fulfilment of its task by each individual constituent part: "You are built upon the foundation laid by the apostles and prophets, and Christ Jesus is the foundation-stone. In him the whole building is bonded together and grows into a holy temple in the Lord. In him you too are being built with all the rest into a spiritual dwelling for God."[17]

This enlargement by Paul of the bride and bridegroom metaphor, this rich juxtaposition of the metaphors of bride, body and building, this massive 'ecumenical' doctrine of the Church emerged from the thinking of a man whose primary purpose in writing the documents which contain these ideas was evangelistic and *pastoral*.

Again and again the emphasis is *ethical*. Because the Church stands to Christ as a Temple to its foundation, as a Body to its head, as a Bride to her husband, therefore, the inference is drawn, not that the Church's nature is of a particular kind, not that its structure is of a particular pattern, but rather that its duty is to behave in a particular way, its privilege to receive the grace which will enable it to fulfil its particular destiny in the high calling of God in Christ Jesus its Lord.[18]

It was as the apostle saw how absolutely necessary was the contribution which one convert had to make to another, and, no less, the contribution which one congregation had to make to another, that his vision of the Church grew and its central place as a part of the Gospel impressed itself upon him. Being "in Christ" was not only a personal experience, it was a corporate one.[19] To say "we possess the mind of Christ"[20] is, by the very use of the plural "we", to dismiss any idea of individual superiority, and to give expression to the fact that the fullness of truth is found within the Body. The Church is the organ of insight. As W. H. Auden said, using the metaphor of music: "When men are truly brothers, they sing not in unison but in harmony." We only reach our full humanity when we live fully corporately.

Further, we only make our full contribution to *society* when we live, think, and act corporately. History provides us with many illustrations of the effectiveness of such corporate action in pursuit of truth and of justice. We need mention only one such. William Wilberforce,

'God's politician' as he has been called, in a long life dedicated to the eradication of social injustice through parliamentary action, was at the centre of a group of men of considerable influence. His close friend, Henry Thornton, bought a big house at Clapham, only four miles from Westminster. His large library became the 'cabinet room' in which they, together with friends, some of them living in the neighbourhood and others who came to stay for a period, planned a strategy which was to affect the life of the whole nation. Indeed their influence spread to many other parts of the world. By means of consultation over a period of many years, they sought, and found, the mind of Christ, and then, in the hurly burly of parliamentary life and often against the opposition of big business, brought that mind to bear on social ills and selfish ends. One historian has commented: "No Prime Minister had such a cabinet as Wilberforce could summon to his assistance." The minds of the men in this group ranged out widely, and their corporate action led to the welfare of millions.

David Newsome refers to William Wilberforce as "the revered leader of that group of Evangelical philanthropists, later to be nicknamed 'The Clapham Sect', pledged to drive vice out of London society, slavery off the face of the earth, and – among a hundred other laudable objects – to render the enthusiasm of the more rugged pioneers of the Evangelical revival acceptable to the Established Church."[21] Clapham was "for some twenty years the power-house of the Evangelical revival where, together with his like-minded friends and neighbours, he had launched the projects and created the organisation which were to convert Evangelicalism into a national force."[22] "By the time he reached old age, Wilberforce "had become in a sense the conscience of England."[23] He proved that one man can change his times, but to do so he needs the support of a stalwart body of allies.

We Westerns would do well to listen to our African brothers and to balance our exaggerated stress on individualism by their emphasis on the corporate. "Whereas Descartes spoke for Western man when he said *'cogito ergo sum'* – I think, therefore I exist – Akan man's ontology is *'cognatus ergo sum'* – I am related by blood, therefore I exist, or I exist because I belong to a family."[24] Baptised into Christ, we find ourselves belonging to a new solidarity, and the enrichment is beyond all words. We are members of a community which is at once the sign, the instrument, and the foretaste of God's kingdom.[25] The Church, in the words of Karl Barth, is "God's provisional demonstration of his intention for all humanity".

We have seen something of the meaning of baptism in this connection earlier in this book. Paul underlined that teaching, and thereby underlined the importance of baptism, in a remarkable passage in his first letter to the Corinthians. He had been giving a list of some who will not "possess the kingdom of God". He went on: "Such were some of you: but ye were washed, but ye were sanctified, but ye were justified in the name of the Lord Jesus Christ, and in the Spirit of our God."[26] I have given the translation of the Revised Version, which brings out the force of the three-fold 'but' in a way that some other translations fail to do. In that 'but' we see the contrast between the life of the unregenerate man and that of the man baptised into Christ. The reference to Christ's cleansing of the Church "by water and word"[27] would seem clearly to have a baptismal connotation ('water'), while 'word' may refer to the liturgical formula, 'in the name of the Lord Jesus'.

Paul's seminal passage on the other sacrament, that of the Eucharist, has an *ethical* setting again. In his first letter to the Corinthians, he gives us what is the earliest account in the New Testament of the institution of the Lord's Supper.[28] The occasion of the giving of that teaching was an unedifying situation in the church at Corinth in which some of the wealthier members of the congregation, leaving work early, came to a communal meal, ate too much and drank too much, leaving others

176

to go hungry and shaming the poorer members of the community. This was no setting for the solemnly joyful celebration of a divinely instituted event! It was an obvious instance of a failure in discernment – a discernment of the Body – and had led to sickness among the members of the community and even to a certain number of deaths.[29] It must not be allowed to continue – such "meetings do more harm than good". The Body of Christ must be treated with reverence and awe.

The Church of Christ in Corinth had gone astray at this crucial point of its liturgical and ethical life. It was but one of many instances of sin within the body of Christian believers. Paul dealt with these matters with a down-to-earth realism – divisiveness,[30] immaturity,[31] sexual immorality,[32] lawsuits among brethren;[33] and so the list could be continued. He had no starry-eyed concept of a perfect Church – *simul justi et peccatores*, at once justified and sinners, that was the fact of the case. A perfect Church must wait for a future age. Meanwhile, the burden of "the care of all the churches"[34] lay heavy on his shoulders, the heavier for the scandal caused by the sins and failures and shortcomings of those churches.

For just as there is a "scandal of the cross", so there is also a scandal of the Church. The cross is "a stumbling block to Jews and folly to Greeks",[35] and this must be faced frankly and the cost of it assessed and accepted realistically. So also with the scandal of the Church. The body of Jesus, as it hung on the cross, was dirty and bloody and full of pain. The Body of Christ, as it goes about its work in the world, is also dirty and bloody and full of pain. It is not for the followers of the Crucified to avoid the shame of the Church, any more than it is for them to avoid the shame of the cross. To shrink from identification with it, to seek to found a perfect Church and so to increase the Church's divisions, or to denigrate before the world the Church of which we are members, is to avoid the scandal of the Church. We weep over its sin and failure. We lament its divisions, its immoralities, its signs of immaturity. But we do so, as Paul did, *from within*, totally at one with it in our own sinfulness and weakness, sharing the shame, accepting the scandal, for we, "washed, sanctified, justified" as we are, still find ourselves dirty and bloody and full of pain. To seek to avoid the implications of that paradox is to flee from the path of the cross. The God "to whom all hearts are open, all desires known, and from whom no secrets are hidden" has no illusions about his Church. He knows its sinfulness and failures but, in spite of all, has never abandoned it nor ever will. For he is love, and love never gives up or despairs. "To say that God is love is to say that he is the entirely disillusioned one."[36] It behoves the members of his Church to follow his example.

But we cannot end here. For though there was for Paul a scandal of the Church – a scandal he never sought to evade – there was also for the apostle an immense strength in the Church, a strength without which it would have been quite impossible for him to do his work and fulfil his mission. The Acts of the Apostles and the letters of Paul himself make this abundantly clear.

It was a member of the church at Damascus who had the courage to welcome him and the graciousness to call him 'my brother'. It was within the fellowship of that same church that he regained his sight and began the process of sorting out the implications, for himself and for the world, of the vision which had so recently come to him. It was that same church which saved his life, when a plot was being hatched against him,[37] and a similar deliverance was brought about by the Church at Lystra when Jews from Antioch and Iconium, having stoned Paul, dragged him out of the city, thinking that he was dead.[38] It was the church in Antioch in Syria which sent Paul and Barnabas on their way,[39] and that same church in Antioch which sent them both to the all-important council at Jerusalem.[40] The church was the sending body, as it was the supporting body, on whose prayers Paul depended for help and strength – he would not set out on the long journey to Spain without calling in at Rome to enjoy the company of his friends there, to receive their support and to enlist their prayers.[41]

It was as a member of the Church, the Bride of Christ, the Body of Christ, the building of the Holy Spirit, as a man baptised, sent, and supported by the Church, that he went on his errands of evangelism and pastoral care. Paul the revolutionary was a member and a leader of a revolutionary *corps*.

MAN OF VISION

Of You we must ask, in You we must seek, at You we must knock. Thus only shall we receive, thus shall we find, thus will it be opened to us.

Augustine: *Confessions*

"Hear, O Israel, the Lord is our God, the Lord is One." From this everything else derives. If God is one, then unity must be of the essence of his creation. It is a fundamental principle of Judaism, confirmed rather than weakened by microscope and telescope alike, that the universe itself is one. So, too, is mankind, for the brotherhood of man is another corollary of belief in the unity of God.

W. W. Simpson: *Jewish Prayer and Worship: An Introduction for Christians*

Life is a glorious road which leads to incomparable splendour, to the very life of God, to the goal of all things, to the full fruition of all that our hearts hold within them.

Abbé de Tourville: *Letters of Direction*

He was "convinced that God was on the side of that which comes rather than on that which goes".

Evelyn Underhill, writing of the Abbé de Tourville

MAN OF VISION

When we were considering "the harvest of the Spirit", we noticed that 'hope' does not occur in the list in Galatians 5: 22–3.[1] Nevertheless, it was a major constituent in Paul's ethical teaching, part of his great trinity of "faith, hope and love"[2] – the joy of expectation in this life and in the life to come. We must develop this a little further, first, in its personal aspects and then in its cosmic outreach.

At the end of his great chapter on the Resurrection, Paul is celebrating Christ's victory over death. Death's victory is no more – Christ has won! Death's sting has been drawn – Christ is risen! "God be praised, he gives us the victory through our Lord Jesus Christ."[3] So, when the possibility of imminent martyrdom faced him, he found himself confronted with a choice between two courses, both of them good. One was to "stay on in the body" (that would mean continued pastoral care for the members of the Philippian church and others). The other was "to depart and be with Christ; *that is better by far*", for to him "life is Christ, and death gain".[4] Here we see the outworking, in personal terms, of the victory over death which was at the heart of Paul's gospel.

We can watch the apostle taking this further in a remarkable passage in his second letter to the Corinthians.[5] Paul no doubt found it as difficult as we do to speak of the realities of death, dying, and "what is after dying", but here he makes a brave attempt. He faces us with the seen and the unseen, with the temporal and the eternal. When he comes to think of his own body, battered by storms and beatings and sickness, he knows that it will not serve him much longer, tough though that body has been. The "earthly frame" will soon be ready for "demolition". But that will not be the end. God has provided a building, "a house not made by human hands, eternal, and in heaven". In the here and now, two processes are in operation. One is the steady, and observable, decline of physical powers. The other is the simultaneous renewal of our spiritual personalities. So – with a slight change of imagery – Paul sees himself, when his earthly frame is sloughed off, not going out into 'nakedness' (might we say 'nothingness'?), but being "absorbed into life immortal", having a "heavenly habitation put on over this one". Language and imagery are strained to express what it means when we speak of death being swallowed up in victory. But the essence of it all is that, having left "our home in the body", we "go to live with the Lord". This is the point which he reached in writing to the Philippians – "to depart" is "to be with Christ". The great reality of being "in Christ" here cannot be undone by the incident of mere physical dissolution. Here is the very essence of personal Christian hope. "We know that he who raised the Lord Jesus to life will . . . bring us to his presence" (4: 14).

But Paul could not rest content with thinking in terms of personal life-fulfilment only. As he looked around him at the world in which he travelled so widely, he saw a world dominated by the immense power-structure of Rome and fertilised by the wisdom of Greece. Its towns and cities were peppered with shrines and temples – the citizens had "gods many and lords many".[6] And yet he found himself compelled to describe them as "without hope and without God" in the world.[7] For the knowledge of God as Paul himself knew him in Christ was not yet theirs, and the hope of the consummation of all things in Christ had not been seized by them. Writing to the Corinthians, he found himself compelled to refer to the "governing powers" as "declining to their end". For all its outward magnificence, the existing order had within it the seeds of decay, precisely because it was relying on human wisdom and human achievement rather than on the revelation made to man in Christ, himself the wisdom of God and the power of God.[8]

Was this a kind of sick pessimism on the part of the apostle? Or was it not, rather, the result of a prophetic insight into the reality of things? Centuries might pass before the power of Rome finally fell before the onslaught of the invaders and Augustine had to write his work on the abiding *City of God*. But the seeds of decay had long been at work, and the insight of Paul was such that he could not engage in an easy philosophy of gradual social improvement till Utopia was finally achieved. The biblical view of history has always been more at home when it moves in areas of conflict, tragedy and apocalyptic judgement than when it expresses itself in terms of gradual improvement and human perfectionism. And who is to say that the realism of Christianity is not corroborated by the witness of history? The new civilisation proclaimed by the Soviet Union ends in the prison-camps of the Gulag Archipelago; the theories of racial superiority end in the mass graves of Auschwitz, the horrors of Sharpeville, and the tortures of Latin American nations; and even the carefully laid plans of Western welfare-states seem to be producing peoples so enfeebled that they cannot defeat the threats of violence without and of moral deterioration within.

Against the dark back-cloth of human tragedy as he saw it around him, Paul set about his work, founding and supporting churches whose members were "like stars in a dark world", proferring "the word of life".[9] The very darkness of the world served as a stimulus to him to spread the light. But in addition to this work of present missionary strategy, his mind ranged out into the future, seeking to see its outline in the light of God's acts in Christ and of his powerful presence by the Spirit. He began to see a vision of the End, the great climax towards which the universe was moving, when God's mission, initiated in creation and renewed in redemption, would reach that transcendent unity which God

185

wills for his whole creation. Nothing short of that vision of a great consummation when God would be "all in all" would satisfy the apostle.

For Paul took *history* seriously. He was in the succession of men like Isaiah, Jeremiah and Habakkuk, who, amid the clash of conflicting cultures, could discern the guiding hand of One who was in history "both creatively and redemptively, creating all that was good in it and redeeming all that was evil and mistaken".[10] Human and cosmic history was to Paul the scene in which God operates, working out with immense patience his plan till it reaches its victorious conclusion. Teilhard de Chardin liked to think of God not so much as the God *above* as the God *ahead*, pulling the whole of evolution towards himself. It was a symbol which greatly appealed to him. Though Paul necessarily thought in categories very different from those of a palaeontologist such as de Chardin, the overall concept of a God always moving ahead on to the End was totally congenial to him.

Further, Paul took the ideas of *sin and death* seriously. Teilhard de Chardin has been criticised for his lack of attention to sin, which he tended to speak of in terms of the "waste product of evolution". Over against this, it can be seen from his writings that he took with great seriousness the element of conflict and of struggle in human progress; after all, he lived through two world wars – he died in 1955. In the case of Paul there is no shadow of doubt about the seriousness with which he regarded sin and its "wages", death,[11] nor the frustration and the shackles of mortality under which creation labours – indeed, "the whole created universe groans in all its parts as if in the pangs of childbirth", a groaning in which Christians also share.[12]

But, above these grim realities of sin and death which he treated with stark realism, was another and greater reality: Paul took *God* seriously. Though he did not put it in these terms, he believed that God, having set his hand to the creation of his universe, would not look back till his purpose in and for that creation was realised. "The created universe waits . . ." "We, to whom the Spirit has been given . . . wait."[13] We live in the era of "not yet", of hope so far only partially fulfilled; but we live in the knowledge that God is co-operating for good with those who love him, who cannot be separated from his love by any power in the universe.[14] On the grand scale, Paul saw the *universe*, created through Christ and for Christ, reconciled through Christ to the Father.[15] He who is the "Source, Guide, and Goal of all that is"[16] will be "all in all", the Son himself "subordinate to God who made all things subject to him".[17] The theme is stated, majestically, in the Epistle to the Ephesians: "He has made known to us his hidden purpose . . . to be put into effect when the time was ripe: namely, that the universe, all in heaven and on earth, might be brought into a unity in Christ."[18]

Meanwhile, in this era of the "not yet", God has given us, in the person of Christ, a foretaste and a pledge of his triumph over death and of the final consummation of the End. The Resurrection of Christ is God's 'No' to the menace of sin and death; his 'Yes' to the final victory. In his Bampton Lectures, Dr A. R. Peacocke gives us some of the implications of what God was unveiling in Jesus the Christ:

The man Jesus existed in the world as we do; he was made of carbon, nitrogen, oxygen, and so on, as we are. His body bore all the marks of its evolutionary history, as ours do . . . He, too, like us, represented an apparently temporary configuration of the stuff of the world – but a configuration which thinks, loves, and knows itself, as we do. In himself, as man, he (like us) represented the fundamental mystery, glory, and tragedy of persons emergent in a physical cosmos. Yet his openness to God – to the point of offering not only his life, but also his relationship to God itself to God to fulfil his purposes – was the occasion and opportunity for that unveiling of God's action on behalf of man we call the resurrection. In that action those who had known the human person of Jesus became convinced that he had in all his human personhood been taken through death, with all its dissolution and apparent reversion to primeval chaos, into a new mode of life within the very being of the God who transcends all matter – energy – space – time. In what happened to Jesus then, we have to say that God has, as it were, unmistakably shown his hand, has unveiled further his purposes in the cosmos and the meaning he has written in man.[19]

This concept of Christ as the foretaste and pledge of the great consummation, the end to which all creation moves, cannot be something peripheral in Paul's scheme of things. The ultimate triumph of God is the coping-stone without which the building would have about it an element of the ridiculous. The strength of J. Christiaan Beker's recent book, *Paul the Apostle: The Triumph of God in Life and Thought*, is that he compels us to face the central place which the apocalyptic element occupies in the teaching of Paul. He goes so far as to say that "apocalyptic is the indispensable means for his interpretation of the Christ-event",[20] and he works this out in its relation to the main themes of Paul's theology. From his fine closing chapter entitled "The Triumph of God", I quote a few sentences which indicate a little of the close bearing of this integral strand of Paul's teaching on the task of the Church and the life and witness of the Christian:

God's love in Christ opens the horizon of the future consummation: "all things" (Rom. 8: 32b) refers to the final defeat of the powers (Rom. 8: 38–9) and our total communion with God in the new age.[21] The sufferings of this world are not a dark foil for the glory of Christian life in separation from the world but a mark of Christian solidarity with the world . . . In the light of God's coming triumph, the world's sufferings become for us a new task.[22] The End, announced in Christ, manifests the eternal faithfulness of the God of the Beginning. Because of his eschatological triumph in Christ, he is indeed the God who rules history from the beginning and demands our absolute trust . . . Our life and all of creation rest securely in the hand of the God who through the tears of suffering will provide the joy of our glory and so bless the seeming futility and pain of the created order.[23]

"The universe brought into a unity in Christ." We noted the phrase in the first chapter of the letter to the Ephesians. Paul writes in this letter primarily of the Church; but here his thought moves out far beyond it, to the sphere where "principalities and powers" engage, where spiritual battles are fought and issues decided. To a modern man, the term 'universe' conveys something very different from what it did to Paul, into whose thinking such concepts as evolution and light-years had never entered. Even in terms of space and time, Paul's 'universe' was a tiny thing compared with ours. But I venture to think that he would have responded with excitement to such a passage as this which I take from a modern writer who is doing much to interpret the world of modern science to that of theology and vice-versa: the universe

is structured and ordered throughout in accordance with the principle of the primacy of light which God has given it from its very beginning. The immense extent of the universe, judged by the time it takes rays of light to traverse it at the fantastic speed of about 186,000 miles per second, is utterly over-whelming. Judged by the same standard, the finite speed of light, the universe is finite, yet since it is found to be continuously expanding at a rate approaching the speed of light, it is also unbounded in a double sense: it extends its boundaries and breaks through the bounds of our comprehension. Nevertheless, it reveals itself throughout to be constituted and flooded by light, which in spite of its vast difference is surely a created reflection of the uncreated and unlimited Light which God himself is.[24]

I imagine Paul reading *The Times* of 2 March, 1981, which reported the discovery by American scientists of three huge, previously unknown galaxies 10,000 million light-years away from earth, the most distant part of the universe yet seen, all three galaxies being far, far bigger than our Milky Way galaxy. He might well have echoed the complaint contained in the title of one of J. B. Phillips' books, *Your God is Too Small*, and would have rejoiced to stretch the bounds of his imagination and his worship – with awe and trembling.

It was left to the writer of the book of the Revelation to set down in considerable detail his vision of the New Jerusalem, the city of God coming down from heaven.[25] He seems to have glimpsed a world community, an open city drawing its wealth from all the nations, illuminated by the glory of God made known in Christ, worshipping God yet without a temple, "for its temple was the sovereign Lord God and the Lamb". His mind moved in ways very different from that of Paul, but in their apprehension of an End, planned by God, to be consummated in Christ, they were in all essentials one.

I have referred to and quoted from Teilhard de Chardin more than once in this book. He found in Paul a highly congenial mind and one whose thought was greatly needed at the time when de Chardin was doing his most creative work. His biographer, Robert Speaight, insists strongly that the foundation of his thought and of his apologetic was Paul:

The tendency of Modernism is to diminish the transcendent stature of Christ: Teilhard's concern was to enlarge it to cosmic proportions. So far from inventing a Christ to fit his own ideas, Teilhard had already found him in St Paul. It was "he in whom all things

190

consist" (Colossians 1: 17); "he who fills all things" (2: 10): "the Christ who is all in all" (3:11); and "has ascended high above all the heavens to fill all things with his presence" (Ephesians 4:10).[26] . . . the cosmic influence of Christ. This was the "universal element", and this was what St Paul had meant by the pleroma; for Christ was not only a head of the body – which was the Church – but the head of all creation.[27]

We began this chapter with some words on hope. We end on that note, too. For it is God's indefeasible purpose to "recapitulate in Christ all the rich possibilities of creation, both those on earth and those in heaven".[28] He who has that hope firmly centred in Christ can never despair.

PAUL AND JESUS

Who hath known the mind of the Lord, that he may instruct him? But we have the mind of Christ.

1 Corinthians 2: 16 (AV)

Let this mind be in you which was also in Christ Jesus ...

Philippians 2: 5 (AV)

Let the word of Christ dwell in you richly in all wisdom.

Colossians 3: 16 (AV)

We discovered ... clear evidence that Paul had leavened his ethical thinking with the great principles enunciated by his Master.

A. M. Hunter: *Paul and his Predecessors*

PAUL AND JESUS

"Wheresoever I open St Paul's epistles, I meet not words but thunder, and universal thunder, thunder that passes through all the world." These words of John Donne, Dean of St Paul's, echo those of Erasmus: "Paul thunders and lightens and speaks sheer flame". If by thunder and lightning and flame these writers mean to convey the ideas of awe and enlightenment and warmth, they undoubtedly describe the effect of Paul's letters on themselves. But this cannot be said to be the experience of all who read his letters – far from it. Indeed, many of his readers are distinctly nervous of him. They would be loath to admit it, but the fact remains. Why should this be so?

If they were to analyse their fear of him, that analysis would have many facets, each depending on the particular personality, background, and outlook of the person concerned. To some, the concepts with which Paul deals in his writings are so grand, so majestic, that the reader feels he is made more for walking in the lowlands than for mountaineering on the heights; Paul is too big for them to take on. To others, his thought-forms, the language which he uses in giving expression to his ideas and convictions, are so foreign to those which they are accustomed to, that the effort to 'translate', to come to terms with them, calls for more mental struggle and energy than they are prepared to give. How *does* one bridge the chasm which yawns between the first century and the twentieth? Between Jew and Gentile? Between a non-scientific age and one that is technologically and scientifically orientated?

But for others the problem takes on a different

aspect – one more subtle and perhaps more profound. To them, it is obvious that the Pauline themes are majestic, but they would be prepared to have a go and take him on. And again, they readily admit that there is a chasm, a big chasm, yawning between the thought-forms and categories of the first century and those of the twentieth; but that would not finally daunt them. After all, Plato and the great 'classic' thinkers and writers propounded their theses in ages as remote from us as Paul's, and more so; but we do not despair of understanding them. On the contrary, they form the basis of much philosophical thinking today. No; the problem goes deeper.

Sometimes the problem is presented in forceful expression; sometimes it scarcely finds words, but none the less it exists as an irritant, rather like a speck of dust which it is hard to locate in a tender and sensitive eye. It could be put at its simplest like this: "We have an uneasy feeling that Paul, if he was not actually disloyal to the teaching of Jesus, at least got it out of focus, at least put the stresses where Jesus did not, complicated the Galilean preaching almost beyond recognition; at worst, gave us 'another' Gospel which is not the Gospel of Jesus as depicted for us by the four Evangelists. We would not go so far as A. N. Whitehead and say: 'the man who . . . did more than anybody else to distort and subvert Christ's teaching was Paul', nor as far as J. S. Mill: 'I hold St Paul to have been the first great corrupter of Christianity'; but isn't there *something* in what they say?"

Let us leave theory on one side for a moment, and root what we are trying to say in the context of parochial life. If we were to say to a group of clergy, "Take your sermon notes of the last five years or so and do a bit of calculating. For our present purpose we need not be concerned with the Old Testament. How many of those sermons were based on the Gospels? How many on Paul's writings?" As between the Gospels and Paul, we would guess that the number of addresses given on the Gospels would *far exceed* those given on Paul. If this is so, why is it? This is a healthy exercise, for it pinpoints some of the questions which we have just raised.

A frank answer to the question would sometimes be that it is easier to put together some thoughts on an incident from the Gospels or on a parable of Jesus than to wrestle with a major Pauline theme – we *all* have an element of laziness in us! Those long and complicated sentences, that severely theological language, those difficult and tortuous bits of exposition which rely heavily on the subtleties of Rabbinic exegesis, contrast so strongly with the apparent (note this adjective 'apparent') simplicities of the parabolic teaching of the young Rabbi from Galilee. But deeper than the matter of laziness lies the niggling but basic question: Did the apostle get it right? Or did he distort it? Is his teaching *authentic* in its exposition of the basic truths of the Master?

To this we must address ourselves, remembering, of course, that in a short space we can only touch on some of the main facets of the subject.

First, we should *expect* to find great differences between Master and apostle. Jesus was a countryman, Paul a man of the big cities, himself a citizen of Tarsus. (Who was it who said that there is hardly a blade of grass in his writings?) Jesus was a non-academic; the local synagogue and the occasional visit to the Temple and its teachers provided him with practically the only source of his official 'education'. Paul was a graduate of Tarsus and of Jerusalem. Jesus used the parabolic method of teaching – reaching mind and heart and will through vivid story and pointed question, seeking a response of 'yes' or 'no' to its total impact. Paul was a theologian, at home in the world of more abstract ideas, though passionately concerned to elicit a response to the Person and the demands of his Lord. All this must be borne in mind. But there is something deeper and far more significant when we consider the differences between Master and apostle.

Jesus fulfilled his ministry of teaching *before* his crucifixion and resurrection. Paul taught and wrote *after* those events. Jesus' teaching was, therefore, anticipatory and forward-looking. Paul's was retrospective so far as the saving events of Good Friday and Easter were concerned. (This is not, of course, to neglect the fact that the Pauline teaching has a strongly 'anticipatory' aspect, for his whole gospel is set in the nexus of his apocalyptic hope.)[1] The heart of Paul's gospel was found in the events which he outlines in 1 Corinthians 15: 3–5: "that Christ died for our sins . . . that he was buried; that he was raised . . . that he appeared . . ." These, for Paul, were life-transforming events. These things, "first and foremost" in his proclamation, had changed the course of history. For Paul, Christ, from henceforth, gave meaning to the universal scheme of things. Paul's stance, therefore, was necessarily different from that of the One who was at the heart of those events. There had taken place a fundamental *shift*. As Günther Bornkamm, admittedly over-simplifying, puts it: "The Gospels tell of Jesus' preaching and work on earth up to the time of his death and resurrection. But with the post-Easter witnesses and the apostolic preaching (Epistles, Acts, Revelation), the death and resurrection are the basis and starting point. The proclaimer has become the subject of proclamation, his life has assumed dimensions that it did not have on earth, and for Jesus' own words are substituted the word about Jesus Christ, his death, resurrection, and second coming at the end of the world."[2] Paul's theology was his answer to the work of God in Christ. He looked back on Christ's finished work and saw that, in his saving deeds and in the fact of Pentecost, God's reign had been initiated and the powers of the new age were now mightily at work. That is why Paul's theology is essentially doxology. This fundamental shift must constantly be borne in mind when we are seeking to understand the differences between Jesus and Paul.

The upbringing and background, then, of Jesus and

Paul were very different. So were the stances from which they looked out on their world. But they were totally at one in the main issues to which they addressed themselves, namely, man's *relationship* to God, to his fellow human beings, and to the world around him. This is the essence of religion – what it is that binds men to God, to men, and to the world; what it is that breaks or mars that 'binding'; how the relationship once broken can be repaired. This is the world in which the religious man moves. This is the world in which Jesus and Paul moved. So Günther Bornkamm writes that Paul's theology is "dominated by the *encounter between God, man and the world* . . . This encounter is the thing to which Paul holds fast in all his thinking."[3] Precisely the same could be said of the teaching of Jesus. Both gave their lives, one in Jerusalem, the other in Rome, because they cared about these relationships more than anything else. If, at *this* point, there is a fundamental difference between Master and apostle, then our doubts about Paul will have real basis. If, at this point, they are found to be essentially in agreement, to cohere, then we shall have to take the writings of the apostle with the utmost seriousness, to wrestle with them, to feed on them, to live by them, to expound them.

Different as were the backgrounds of Jesus and Paul, the two men were the same in this respect – that both were Israelites; theirs were "the covenants, the law, the temple worship, and the promises".[4] Both were nourished from childhood in Jewish homes and educated in Jewish synagogues. Both were taught the sacredness of the law, with its manifold commandments and prohibitions. Both, from childhood, addressed themselves to the basic questions of how a man can be right with God and what it is that breaks a right relationship.

The latter point – the 'defiling' of relationships between men and God – was, understandably enough, a major subject in the Rabbinic schools and in the education of the people. A great deal of space is given to this in the Old Testament, and in the elaboration of rules in later literature, rules which were drawn up to safeguard people against any infringement of the law and against the disasters which must assuredly follow such infringement.

When we come to study the Gospels, it is startling to see how lightly Jesus sat to these rules. Indeed, he went further. He flouted some of them. He "declared all foods clean".[5] The Old Testament had gone to great lengths to declare many foods *unclean*.[6] Jesus touched lepers. He did not seek to avoid contact with a woman with a haemorrhage. He mixed freely with 'unclean' Gentiles. Why this open flouting of the regulations? Because he wanted to teach by his actions, as he did by his words, that the things which break contact with God do not consist in matters of physical contact, but in matters which have their origin in the mind, in desire, in human relationships. A list is given – "evil thoughts, acts of fornication, of theft, murder, adultery, ruthless greed, and malice . . . these things come from inside, and they defile the man."[7]

When we turn to Paul, we find that though, in his youth, he outstripped many of his Jewish contemporaries in his "boundless devotion to the traditions" of his ancestors,[8] when he became a Christian his whole approach altered. He could mix with 'unclean' Gentiles without any scruples; he was unconcerned about whether things were officially clean or not. He felt himself compelled to oppose Peter to the face when the latter, who had grasped the issue at stake and was taking his meals with Gentile Christians, then went back on his new convictions and "began to hold aloof", to "play the Pharisee".[9] Paul knew that Jesus was right. This was no matter of detail. This touched the basic matter of man's relationship with *God*. That does not depend on external 'cleanness' or 'uncleanness'. It does depend on the rightness of a man's heart, his relationship with others, his purity of will.

Jesus and Paul were at one in the matter of what

breaks fellowship. Though that is negative, it is no less important for that.

But, positively, how can a man be right with God? How can a man look up into the face of God and know that all is well? Here, put in monosyllables, is *the* fundamental question of all religion. Let us turn, first, to the teaching of Jesus. After that we shall look at Paul's. We shall, for the present purpose, confine ourselves mainly to the Gospel according to Luke and to six passages therein.

(i) Luke 4, 14–30

His baptism and temptation behind him, Jesus returned to his home town of Nazareth and, in the synagogue on the Sabbath day, stood up to read the lesson. It was from Isaiah 61. As he read this passage of 'liberation theology' – good news to the poor, release for prisoners, recovery of sight for the blind and freedom for victims, and as he applied this to himself – the people heard what was in fact an outline of the ministry that Jesus intended to exercise. A gasp of delight went up from the congregation. They had never realised that religion could be like that – so intimately related to life in its extremities of need, so forceful, so loving, so strong. Indeed, they were listening to "words of grace". Then Jesus began to apply the passage. He looked back over Israel's history. He quoted two instances of how God's saving health reached not Israel, his 'chosen' people (for they were unbelieving), but Gentiles, 'outsiders', a widow from Sidon territory, a Naaman, an army commander from Syria. But this sounded monstrous to the men in the synagogue that day. The *Jews* were God's people. His covenant-relationship was with *them*. To say that God's grace and goodness were equally available to all made nonsense of their privileges. And "they leapt up, threw him out of the town, and took him to the brow of the hill . . . meaning to hurl him over the edge." Equal access, equal grace, for all? That was what Jesus declared. They could not take it.

What he declared that day in his exposition of Isaiah 61 he was to work out in life when he met the need of a Roman centurion in response to his faith,[10] and answered the audacity of a Gentile woman, a Phoenician of Syria.[11] The traditional Jewish idea of a chosen people was shattered. The kingdom of Heaven was open to all believers. "From east and west people will come, from north and south, for the feast in the kingdom of God. Yes, and some who are now last will be first, and some who are first will be last."[12]

(ii) Luke 7: 36–50

In this passage we have two stories, the one folded inside the other. The 'outside' story is that of the Pharisee who invited Jesus to dinner. The host and, no doubt, the guests were shocked that a woman, notorious for her evil living, came and poured out her grateful devotion at the feet of Jesus. Jesus perceived that the Pharisee resented the woman's action and that he was thinking that, had Jesus known what sort of woman was kissing his feet, he would have turned her away.

Now comes the 'inside' story which Jesus told. There were two debtors, one of whom owed a huge sum, the other a paltry one; but both of them were equally powerless to repay a single silver piece. The creditor, out of sheer grace, forgave them both. Which of the two would love him most? The one to whom most was forgiven, of course. Jesus lodges the lesson firmly in the Pharisee's conscience, and then turns to the woman: "Your sins are forgiven," he says. "Your faith has saved you. Go into peace."

Three major religious themes meet in this passage – grace, faith, and peace. "He *graced* them both"; that is the literal translation of the verb. ("He frankly forgave them both", AV; "he generously cancelled both of their debts", J. B. Phillips.)

"Your *faith* has saved you" (v.50). The woman had nothing to offer but the gratitude which overflowed from her heart. Her "faith" was her response to the "grace" of Jesus. It rescued her from a life of despair and allowed her to leave behind a life of shame and bitterness and to go into *peace*. Where divine grace and the human response of faith meet, there life begins. Peace enters the personality; integration and wholeness grow.

(iii) Luke 10: 30–7

The parable of the Good Samaritan is frequently misunderstood. "Be kind to other people, especially those in need; that is what Christianity is all about" – so it is generally interpreted. But it goes far deeper than this. The basic question at issue is: how to inherit eternal life. The lawyer put the question. Jesus replied by quoting the commandment of love to God and neighbour, but it did not satisfy the questioner, who wanted to vindicate himself. It was in reply to his further question, "Who is my neighbour?", that Jesus told the parable.

Two points must be noted. First, that Jesus showed that, where there was a case of need, the question of giving and receiving mercy transcended national and racial barriers. In this instance of highway robbery, those who might have been expected to come to the rescue because they belonged to specially 'religious' groups, failed to do so – it was safer to look the other way! The man whose compassion showed itself in risk and expenditure of time and of money was a Samaritan, hated by the Jews and regarded by them with the greatest distaste and suspicion.

The second point is of even greater importance. Bishop F. C. N. Hicks put it succinctly: "The lawyer is bidden to see himself in the picture as the man by the roadside: naked, wounded, starving. He must learn that he must first be clothed, healed, housed and fed. Then, not from a pedestal of superiority, but as one who has himself repented, and suffered, and received all that he

203

has that is worth having, he can go and do good to others."[13]

(iv) Luke 15: 11–32
Kenneth E. Bailey has written a remarkable and all-too-little-known book entitled *The Cross and the Prodigal*. The author served in the Middle East for ten years and talked at length with pastors, elders and illiterate farmers. He has thus been enabled to look at the parables of Jesus through their eyes, understanding, as it is hard for Westerners to do, the underlying assumptions and the subtleties of allusion and of humour in the stories. These things have changed but little in the course of two or three millennia. To understand such a story as that of the Prodigal Son, it is essential to lay aside our Western spectacles, difficult as that may be. Bailey helps us to do so.

In the course of his work in the Near East, Bailey found himself faced with a problem put by his Moslem friends. "Christians" – for our purpose in this book we might say Paul – "have perverted the message of Christ. The story of the Prodigal Son proves that the cross is unnecessary to forgiveness. The boy comes home. His father welcomes him. There is no cross and no incarnation. Islam with no cross or saviour preserves the true message of Christ."[14]

Not so, says Bailey. The cross is implicitly present in the story. "The suffering of the cross was not primarily the physical torture but rather the agony of rejected love,"[15] – an agony which goes on all through the estrangement, an agony of which the son is quite unaware. This is the way of God with man on Golgotha. "God was in Christ reconciling the world to himself."

When the son reaches home, he finds a father ready to "kiss him again and again" (v.20) and to reinstate him; to robe him in his own robe (the father's); to give him a ring which indicates authority in the house, and shoes which betoken his sonship (a slave would be barefoot).

What can the son do but blurt out his own unworthiness – "I am no longer worthy to be called your son"? He puts himself completely at the mercy of his father. He does not even offer his service ("Make me a hired servant" is a phrase added by a "dull-witted copyist", in v.21). The boy leaves his destiny entirely in his father's hands. The father pays the price of self-emptying love to reconcile the son to himself. The son brings nothing home but a handful of filthy rags. Only the father can restore, and restoration is through grace alone.

To call this story the parable of the prodigal son is a misnomer. *Both* sons were lost – the one who rebelled, kicked over the traces, and went into the far country and to a dissolute life; and the other who, though physically remaining in the father's house, showed himself utterly uncomprehending of the way his father's heart worked. Proud and self-sufficient, scornful of the reality of his brother's conversion, it is the elder brother who, at the end of the story, is left outside, arguing, while the younger, having returned naked and penniless, is within, clothed and rejoicing. The real 'problem-child' is the elder of the two. Arrogance barred the door against love. Physically at home, he was miles away from understanding the 'prodigality' of a father's grace. "It is easier to convert the Prodigal Son than his brother or his uncle who is a professor."[16] The parable leaves us wondering whether, perhaps at long last, the father's outgoing love would penetrate the older son's defences as it had done those of the younger.

(v) Luke 18: 9–14

In this parable of the Pharisee and the tax-gatherer we have two figures brilliantly depicted. The first, the Pharisee, is seen strutting on the stage, parading before the Almighty his good works, activities which went far beyond that which the law demanded. "See what a good boy am I!" The other "kept his distance" from the Temple-stage. Beating his breast, he could only pray:

"O God, have mercy on me, sinner that I am." He had nothing to offer but the sin from which he needed release. But realising that to the full opened up his personality to the reception of God's forgiving grace. "It was this man ... and not the other, who went home acquitted of his sins". He could look up to God and know that all was well.

(vi) Luke 19: 1–10

The story of the little tax-gatherer which begins with his curiosity "to see what Jesus looked like", ends with his "salvation" (v.9). The initiative was with Jesus – *he* made the first move and invited himself to Zacchaeus' house. "The decisive action, contrary to all that would be expected at the time, stemmed from Jesus. Zacchaeus for his part responds with joy ... Salvation comes even to Jews only when Jesus goes after them and brings them home. So the narrative concludes with the great declaration of the task of the Son of man as a shepherd,"[17] come "to seek and save what is lost".

Looking back over this little catena of passages of the teaching of Jesus, we may summarise the main points as follows: The way to rightness with God is open to all, irrespective of nationality or class. The initiative is with God, and issues from his character of outgoing love. His is a prodigality of grace. Human arrogance and pride constitute the main barrier to the reception of that grace. But where faith (of which we shall shortly have more to say) meets divine grace, there life and peace, integration of the whole personality, begin.

We turn now to the teaching of Paul. As he moved about the Graeco-Roman world, both in the centres of Jewish life and in the 'pagan' lands which he visited, as his vigilant eye observed and his keen mind pondered the divisions of mankind, it was clear to him that they were essentially three-fold. As we saw in chapter 8, the barriers which separated men from one another were those of race, class and sex. At the same time as he saw that ugly phenomenon, he saw another, the second as full of hope as the first was marked by despair. He saw a new humanity coming into being, a humanity in which these barriers were transcended, yes, even eliminated. "In Christ", he wrote to the Galatians,[18] "there is no such thing as Jew and Greek" – so the *race* barrier is down; "no such thing as slave and freeman" – so the *class* barrier, the barrier of privilege, is down; "no such thing as male and female" – so the *sex* barrier is down (*exit* chauvinism of all kinds!). In the great announcement which introduces the letter to the Romans, Paul makes it clear at the start that the Gospel is God's saving force for *everyone* who has faith – admittedly for the Jews first, for it was through them that the preparatory work had been done, but also for the Gentiles. Faith, not race, is the criterion of acceptance with God. The status of the person or the colour of the hand that grasps God's grace matters not one whit. "The revelation" is "by eternal God's command made known *to all nations*, to bring them to faith and obedience".[19] As with the teaching of Jesus, so with the teaching of Paul, there can be no shadow of doubt about the universality of the Christian message.

Nor can there be any doubt about Paul's insistence (as Jesus had insisted) that, in the matter of man's relationship with God, the initiative is with *him*. This is the meaning of grace. James Stewart goes so far as to say that Jesus "was the divine initiative incarnate".[20] That is but another way of making John's great affirmation about the Word being made flesh and dwelling among us, full of grace and truth, and Paul would have been more than happy to add his 'yes' to that. God makes the first move. To put it in terms of grammar, the active verb is used of God when the matter of putting a man's relationship right with him is under discussion. God justifies the man who puts his faith in Jesus; he is the one who acquits the guilty; he justifies them and gives them his splendour.[21] God puts us in the right, us who were very much in the wrong.

Bornkamm makes it clear that "Paul's gospel of justification by faith alone matches Jesus' turning to the godless and the lost".[22] In the preaching and activity of Jesus, God's "salvation", his gift of freedom and fullness of life, came as actual experience into the lives of men and women. Jesus encounters them, searches them out, reveals to them their lostness, takes the initiative, and rescues them. Paul, the one-time Pharisee, himself so like the Pharisee in the temple, so like the elder brother (in Luke 15), finds himself confronted by "the divine initiative incarnate" on the Damascus road, sees his spiritual nakedness revealed in the light from heaven, and stretches out empty hands for the grace proffered to him in God's prodigality of love. The barrier of his arrogance and pride falls. Life and peace take the place of death and inner tension. The torn man is integrated. He arises – a man with a gospel.

We must now turn our attention to consider the meaning of *faith*, for it is very clear that this is central to the teaching both of Jesus and of Paul when they are dealing with what we have called (and they certainly considered to be) "*the* fundamental question of all religion", namely, the individual's total wholeness, his right relationship God-wards, man-wards, self-wards.

Looking at the occurrence of the word in the Gospel according to Luke, we notice the story of the paralytic brought by his friends to Jesus. Seeing their *faith*, he says to the man, "Your sins are forgiven."[23] Commenting to the crowd on the approach to him of the centurion, Jesus says, "Nowhere, even in Israel, have I found *faith* like this."[24] And the phrase "your *faith* has saved you" runs like a refrain in a series of restoration stories – the woman at the Pharisee's dinner-party; the woman with the haemorrhage; the grateful leper; and the blind beggar.[25]

A glance at a lexicon will show how absolutely central is this word to the thinking of Paul. If we eliminate the few instances where he uses it with the ethical sense of "faithfulness" or "reliability" (as, for example, in his list in Galatians 5: 22), or in the sense of "the Gospel message" (as, for example, in Galatians 3: 23), we are left with the vast majority of cases where he wants to convey the idea of *"that in man which goes forth to lay hold on the offered mercy of God"*.[26] I instance three cases out of many: "He shall gain life who is justified through faith"; God "is himself just and also justifies any man who puts his faith in Jesus"; "by grace you have been saved, through faith; and this is not your own doing, it is the gift of God".[27] *Sola fide*, "by faith alone", is a theme regnant in Paul. To say this, and to say it with full emphasis, is not to ignore the warning which Professor G. W. H. Lampe gave: "It is . . . clear enough that 'faith alone' means 'faith without works of merit'. It does not mean faith without sacraments, nor a subjective and individualistic adherence to Christ which ignores the Church."[28]

James Stewart, in a footnote to his fine book *A Man in Christ*, comments that Paul "could write scarcely a page without some reference to faith". He goes on to define it as "utter self-abandonment to the God revealed in Jesus Christ".[29] That is getting close to the heart of the matter. He quotes by way of example the great affirmation in Galatians: "The life which I now live in the flesh, I live by the faith of the Son of God",[30] and again: "Not having mine own righteousness, which is of the law, but that which is through faith of Christ".[31] (The genitives here are what Deissmann calls "mystic genitives, conveying the sense of personal relationship".) Here, in faith, is a moral and spiritual union of personalities. As Martin Luther put it: "all that is his becomes mine; all that is mine becomes his".

Let two writers, more recent than Luther, help us further. Joachim Jeremias writes: "Faith . . . is the hand which grasps the work of Christ and holds it out to God. Faith says: Here is the achievement – Christ died for me on the cross (Galatians 2: 20). This faith is the only way to obtain God's grace."[32] P. T. Forsyth writes: Faith is "the grand venture in which we commit our whole soul and future to the confidence that Christ is not an illusion but the reality of God."[33] And this it is which leads to *peace*, the kind of peace of which Jesus spoke when he said, "Go into peace", and Paul when he wrote, "We have peace with God through our Lord Jesus Christ."[34]

For peace is the end of hostilities. No longer do we say: "We will not have this man to reign over us."[35] On the contrary, we yield our allegiance to his love. But peace is more than this. Peace is positive harmony between ourselves and God; harmony between ourselves and our neighbours; harmony between the hitherto warring elements in our own character and personality. It is total integration.

We have seen that Jesus and Paul are essentially at one in their teaching about what it is that breaks man's fellowship with God and what it is that restores that broken relationship. Let us take one other aspect of this, the central theme of religion at its deepest, and see whether here there is a radical difference or an essential unity. We refer to their teaching about the Fatherhood of God.

This doctrine is not, of course, peculiar to the New Testament.

In the Old Testament, God is the Father of Israel in the sense that he is the founder and creator of the nation (Deuteronomy 32: 6; Isaiah 63: 16; Malachi 2: 10) . . . The reference . . . is to a particular historical event in the deliverance of the people from Egypt. Thus the act by which Jehovah becomes the Father of Israel is to be thought of as adoption rather than creation. He is the creator of all the peoples; but Israel is in a special sense his son (Hosea 11: 1), even his firstborn (Exodus 4: 22; Jeremiah 31: 9).[36]

When we come to the New Testament, a close study of the teaching of Jesus makes it clear that he speaks of the Father-son relationship in a much more personal way, almost, one might say, in an exclusive manner. The Lord's Prayer, with its intimate beginning, is essentially a *family* prayer for use by those who dare to pray "thy kingdom come, thy will be done", with all the searching implications of those two clauses.

We owe a debt of gratitude to Jeremias for the work he has done on the way in which Jesus used the word *Abba* when addressing God.[37] He maintains that his use of the word has no parallel in the liturgical or the informal prayers of Judaism. Jesus apparently habitually used it when he prayed – the only exception given in the Gospels is the cry from the Cross, "My God, my God, why hast thou forsaken me?"[38] and that is a quotation from Psalm 22: 1. "It was something new, something unique and unheard of, that Jesus dared to take this step and to speak with God as a child speaks with his father, simply, intimately, securely."[39] "*Abba* . . . is a word which conveys revelation. It represents the centre of Jesus' awareness of his mission." And it is to his *disciples*, not to the world in general, that Jesus gives the authorisation to invoke God as *Abba*, thus letting them participate in his own communion with God.[40] If we, rightly, call the *Pater Noster* the Lord's Prayer, it is also rightly called the disciple's prayer. It cannot, in this intimate sense, be called the world's prayer.

In the writings of Paul, we twice meet the word *Abba* again – strangely so, for he wrote in Greek (the almost universal language of the Graeco-Roman world) and *Abba* is Aramaic. The reason for his retention of the Aramaic word is not far to seek. It was so precious a word, coming straight from the lips of Jesus, that he could not abandon it. He held on to it, even though he had at once to translate it – "*Abba*, Father". He used it, in both passages, in the context of the Christian family. It is "because you are *sons*", it is because the Spirit of the Son has been sent "into your hearts", that the word *Abba* can be used.[41] It is as sons of God, moved by his Spirit, that you do not relapse into that state of slavery

211

in which previously you existed, but are now enabled to cry out "*Abba*".[42] This passage from Romans 8 is to be seen in a baptismal context. The baptismal candidates have gone down into the waters, died, come up into newness of resurrection-life, and the first thing they do is to cry out, jubilantly, exultingly, "*Abba*, Father"! They are in the family! Not only is this passage a baptismal one. It is also a trinitarian one. *Jesus*, the Son par excellence, used the word *Abba*. The *Spirit* enables us to use it. So we approach the *Father* with confidence. "We are bold to say 'Our Father'", as the ancient liturgies had it.

> This discovery [says T. A. Smail] is a charismatic gift. To know God's fatherhood and our sonship is not the result of theological expertise or of moral achievement, but a free gift of God the Holy Spirit making real within us what Christ has achieved on our behalf ... This is well brought out in the Good News Bible which runs, "God's Spirit joins himself to our spirits to declare that we are God's children", making it clear that our spirit is authentically involved as the locus and recipient of the declaration, but its authority resides in the Holy Spirit. When the Holy Spirit reveals God's fatherhood on the level of our spirit in this way, then it ceases to be dead doctrine that can win at best intellectual assent, but penetrates to the hidden springs of our personality, not merely with emotional warmth but with life-transforming vitality, so that we do not simply know a truth but enter into a conscious relationship with the one whom that truth proclaims.[43]

So Paul gets very close to the inmost religious experience of Jesus here, and to his teaching to his inner circle of disciples. Here certainly we may speak of him as an interpreter of the teaching of Jesus – and that at a point of deepest intimacy.

An anonymous Church father, perhaps Ambrose,

Bishop of Milan (c.339–397), spoke of Paul as "Christ's second eye". He was not far out. Nor was P. T. Forsyth when he called him "the Fifth Evangelist" and added "and we ought to call him the first in point of time and value both";[44] nor Jeremias when he wrote: "It was Paul's greatness that he understood the message of Jesus as no other New Testament writer did. He was the faithful interpreter of Jesus";[45] nor J. C. Beker who asserted, "It was Paul, more than any other early theologian, who opened the way to the doctrinal purity of the gospel".[46] Let the last word be with James Stewart: "His was the loyal mind that preserved Christ's essential Gospel intact for the world; and his the spiritual genius that has enabled the Holy Catholic Church to realise something of the breadth and length and depth and height of the glory of her own eternal Lord." "All the apostle's great central conceptions . . . came to him straight out of the bosom of Jesus' Gospel."[47]

So far, we have been considering the *doctrinal* teaching of Jesus and of Paul. We must add something about their *ethical* teaching.

Let us begin by reminding ourselves that both Jesus and Paul lived lives of intense activity and were daily engaged in the closest contact with their contemporaries. Neither was in any sense a detached academic – Paul could have become one, but his burning sense of mission demanded constant travel among the young churches for its fulfilment.

The amount of space given in the Gospels to record our Lord's healing ministry underlines the fact that his grappling with sin, ignorance and disease was constant and intense. Here he is bringing peace to a distraught 'Legion' – not a man but a mob. There he is straightening a woman with a twisted back. Here he is raising a little girl smitten down with sickness. There he is giving back her son to a widowed woman. Every day brought him into touch with human need.

When we look at the life and activity of Paul, though

we find a different kind of ministry, it is clear that his contact with people must have been about as close as was that of Jesus. In Paul's case, physical restoration does not appear to have been a primary concern in his ministry, though, if occasion called for it, his prayerful healing touch would bring relief to the father of Publius from his fever and dysentry, and others benefited at the same time.[48] A practical man, he saw to it that the distraught sailors had a meal before they abandoned ship and made for the shore.[49] He included healings among the gifts of the Spirit to the Church.[50] He cared about people's physical well-being.

But his contact with people was not primarily along these lines. His greatest concern was to beseech men, in Christ's name, to "be reconciled to God",[51] and then, having established little Christian nuclei, to build them up into vigorous and self-propagating parts of the Catholic Church. So it was that he had constant and close contact with all sorts and conditions of men and women, Christians and pagans, babes in Christ and mature disciples, human nature redeemed and unredeemed. He was a travelling evangelist, glorying in situations where he saw growth in love and knowledge, wrestling with sin and stupidity, with backsliding and folly in churches where growth was slow and apostasy an ever-present peril.

We should expect, then, to find both in the teaching of Jesus and in that of Paul a strong emphasis on conduct and clear teaching on ethics. This is precisely the case. It would have been impossible for Jesus to train the twelve and to care for the total welfare of those whom he healed, or for Paul to build up Christian communities in the Graeco-Roman world, without their giving strong leadership about conduct. It is very interesting to see how close are the parallels between the teaching of Master and apostle.

Nowhere is this teaching closer than on the primary importance which both assign to *love*. Jesus was approached by one of the Pharisees with a test question:

"Which is the greatest commandment in the Law?" The answer was clear and unequivocal: " 'Love the Lord your God with all your heart, with all your soul, with all your mind.' That is the greatest commandment. It comes first. The second is like it: 'Love your neighbour as yourself.' Everything in the Law and the prophets hangs on these two commandments."[52] The life of Jesus was an outworking of that great saying – his love of the Father finding expression in his passion to do his will even to his death on the cross, and exhibiting itself in a ministry of constant compassion to those in need, whatever their race or social standing.

When we turn to Paul, we think, naturally enough, of his superb hymn to love in 1 Corinthians 13. But in Romans 13: 8–10, his emphasis on love of one's neighbour is so close to that of our Lord in the passage to which we have just referred as to make it probable that, even if he had no written record of what Jesus had said, he had heard it reported by those who had been present when Jesus spoke. E. C. Hoskyns and Noel Davey have summed it up well: "When the good works that St Paul requires of the Christians are analysed, they are seen to be identical with those attributed by the evangelists to Jesus, for they too can be summed up in the one word 'love': 'He that loveth his neighbour hath fulfilled the law . . .' "[53]

Jesus in fullest measure, Paul not so perfectly but nevertheless in great measure, knew love as a divine power operative within them – a reality inaugurated and opened up by God, available to men, flooding "our inmost heart through the Holy Spirit he has given us".[54] It is God who awakens love in a human being, and then there is no limit either to the change of character in the person concerned or to the powerful effects of that love in its direction towards others. "This hymn to love", says Lucas Grollenberg writing of 1 Corinthians 13, "could never have been written had Jesus not shown in his life how closely religion, the service of God, was bound up with the service of one's fellow man. Certainly

Jesus is not mentioned here, but we might say that this was unnecessary; in the last resort, it is Jesus himself who speaks here through Paul in language determined by the circumstances of the Corinthians."[55]

Paul, as a Pharisee, had seen this love powerfully at work. "Lord, lay not this sin to their charge", he had heard the dying Stephen pray, as they stoned him while Saul looked on approvingly.[56] The stones broke the body of Stephen. The prayer broke the pride of Paul. That was love at work. "Saul, *my brother*", Ananias had said to the newly converted Paul, and had laid his hands lovingly on the man who up to then had been harassing the Church.[57] That, too, was love at work. If Stephen's dying love had broken his pride, Ananias' welcoming love healed him. No wonder, in the light of experiences such as these, that he gave central place in his teaching to the love of God, which had so permeated men like Stephen and Ananias and had flooded his own heart.

Only rarely in his writings does Paul speak of man loving God – here he differs from the author of the Johannine literature. Paul prefers to lay his accent on the mighty love of God for us and, when he wishes to speak of our response to that love, to use the word 'faith'. For faith, as we have seen earlier in this chapter, is man's response to God's initial outgoing in love.

It would be possible to engage in a detailed study of the close parallels between the ethical teaching of Jesus and that of Paul, but that would go beyond the scope of this book. We may mention, in passing, their teaching on *retaliation*: Jesus: "Do not set yourself against the man who wrongs you. If someone slaps you on the right cheek, turn and offer him your left . . ." Paul: "You already fall below your standard in going to law with one another at all. Why not rather suffer injury? Why not let yourself be robbed? . . ."[58] On *freedom from anxiety*: Jesus: "I bid you put away anxious thoughts about food and drink to keep you alive, and clothes to cover your body. Surely life is more than food, the body more than clothes." Paul: "Have no anxiety, but in

216

everything make your requests known to God in prayer and petition with thanksgiving. Then the peace of God, which is beyond our utmost understanding, will keep guard over your hearts and thoughts . . ."[59] *On loving one's enemies*: Jesus: "Love your enemies and pray for your persecutors." Paul: "Call down blessings on your persecutors – blessings, not curses."[60] The list could be continued at length. All the ethical teaching, both of Jesus and of Paul, is the application of the fundamental principle of *love* to the varied circumstances and problems thrown up by life and discipleship.

"The only thing that counts", says Paul in a powerful sentence, "is faith active in love" or, "faith inspired by love".[61] He had found that, when a man dared to expose himself to the incoming grace of God, that very passivity before God was the source of a great new energy in action. Kierkegaard spoke of the Christian religion as "unlimited humiliation, unlimited grace, and unlimited striving out of gratitude." Thomas Erskine put it even more briefly: "Religion is grace, and ethics is gratitude."[62]

INVITATION TO EXPLORATION

Thither we make our way, still as pilgrims, not yet at rest; still on the road, not yet at home; still aiming at it, not yet attaining it.

Augustine: *Sermon 103*

So, with the wan waste grasses on my spear,
I ride forever, seeking after God,
My hair grows whiter than my thistle plume
And all my limbs are loose; but in my eyes
The star of an unconquerable praise;
For in my soul one hope for ever sings,
That at the next white corner of a road
My eyes may look on Him . . .

G. K. Chesterton: *The Wild Knight*

The enterprise
Is exploration into God.
Christopher Fry: *A Sleep of
Prisoners*

I do not ask that men should sing my praises,
Or flaming headlines spread my name abroad,
I only pray that, as I voice the Message,
Men may find God.

INVITATION TO EXPLORATION

It has been the purpose of this book to present Paul as a man of like passions with ourselves, the very opposite of a plaster saint, a man who was compelled to battle with temptations right to the end of his journey; but, at the same time, a man conscious of having been redeemed at great cost, and of being the object of God's transforming grace. We have watched the growth of 'a man in Christ', a 'character' if ever there was one, thinker, writer, pastor, missionary, strategist, man of prayer, fighter, churchman, revolutionary. We have seen a man whose claim to apostleship brooked no denial, but whose chief delight was to be the slave of Jesus Christ and, for the sake of his fellow-Christians, to be their slave too; a man for whom suffering and the loss of all things were irradiated by the confident hope of being 'with Christ' in an intimacy which would transcend his earthly experience. We have seen a man deeply implicated in the tragedies of a world groaning and waiting for deliverance, yet feeling his way towards a vision of God's final triumph over all that is evil, and the consummation of all things in Christ. Paul was a very this-worldly man, but he was an other-worldly man too; and in the maintenance of that paradox of thought and of living, in the stretching of experience almost to breaking point, he grew and never ceased to grow. The implications of the revolution which had taken place in his own life and made him a revolutionary were now seen to be wide as the universe, vast as eternity.

From such a man came the letters, sometimes pouring out in passionate disarray as he struggled to protest against error and to guard the flock entrusted to him;

sometimes achieving a beauty which raised the common language of the people to heights of linguistic excellence; sometimes packed so closely that every phrase, every word, demands our attention as we discover new meaning in passages made familiar by years of repeated reading. In Paul's dynamic rendering of the Gospel, there is that which is "more dangerously explosive and exciting than a cavalry charge".

The words are those of Bernard Levin, writing in *The Times*,[1] not about Paul but about a series of seven recitals given by Alfred Brendel in the Queen Elizabeth Hall, London. He played all the thirty-two sonatas of Beethoven, and Levin described the occasions as a huge and uplifting experience. Back in 1977, he had heard Brendel play the same cycle and had written of it: ". . . Everywhere there is a suggestion of surprise in the playing – so *that's* what Beethoven meant! – which has made me feel that player and audience were sharing a series of discoveries." Levin then went on to speak of the "conviction of absolute authenticity" which conveyed itself in Brendel's rendering of the sonatas in 1983.

Looking back over the series of recitals, Levin wrote:

All the way through we have been transfixed not by the performer's art but by the composer's – the last test, and the most searching of all. Brendel vanishes behind the music; it is almost true to say that if you shut your eyes you miss nothing. What you gain is a journey, in Brendel's company, through Beethoven's genius, a journey of thirty-two milestones on each of which is carved passion, understanding, joy, hope, confidence, beauty, power, together with suffering and darkness and, at the last, a serenity which is not of this world, but which Beethoven has been trusted to bring down to us from his own Sinai of despair defeated . . . Beethoven's ultimate triumph had communicated itself to us with such force and urgency because of the way in which Alfred Brendel played the works.

The parallels between what Brendel did with the works of Beethoven, and what Paul did with the works of God in Christ are extraordinarily close. Put more accurately we might say: Beethoven made an impact on Brendel of the most profound kind, as the disciple sought to interpret the mind of the master. The same result occurred when Paul, grasped by Christ, sought to interpret his person and his mind as he preached, taught and wrote. As we read the writings of Paul we say, often with surprise: "So *that's* what Jesus meant!" We see in Paul's rendering of the Gospel "a conviction of absolute authenticity". And when we get into the very heart of the letters we find ourselves being led into an understanding of the passion, joy, hope, beauty, power, suffering, and serenity of Christ – even into a sharing, by faith, of his ultimate triumph.

The analogy may be pressed further. "All the way through" (the recitals), Levin wrote, "we have been transfixed not by the performer's art but by the composer's – the last test, and the most searching of all. Brendel vanishes behind the music . . ." Brendel had said in the interview that he "did not want to *be in the way* of the composer." Schnabel, in an earlier generation, had told his students much the same thing: "You will only be nervous, when you go to the piano, if you are thinking about yourself. Think of Beethoven, and then *he* will play". Radu Lupu, the distinguished and self-effacing Romanian pianist, maintains that he would rather play to three hundred people who had come to hear the music than to three thousand who had come to hear him.

Professor Owen Chadwick, writing of John Henry Newman as a preacher, made precisely the same point about him and his work as Levin made about Brendel's relationship to Beethoven: "The more overwhelming the reality, the more the preacher's personality started to hide. Popular preachers create their effect by making their personality large. Newman created his effect by disappearing into the reality of which he spoke, as though he must get out of its way."[2]

That was true of Paul, preacher, writer, Christian communicator. Indeed, it was the major reason for his success in these spheres. It was in proportion as he "got out of the way" that success, in the deepest meaning of that much misused word, attended his work. As a man infinitely indebted to Christ, it was his first care "not to get in the way". This cannot have been easy for a man built on such ample proportions. A forceful, dynamic, sometimes abrasive character is not readily hidden. The secret – and he learned it the hard way and by no means always at once – was to "die daily".[3] A daily recognition of himself as having died "to the appeal and power of sin" but being "alive and sensitive to the call of God through Jesus Christ our Lord"[4] was the only way to achieving that end.

The writer of the Fourth Gospel suggests that the motto by which John the Baptist lived was: "He must increase, but I must decrease."[5] The picture in mind may well have been that of a little oil lamp which exists to give light to the surroundings and, having done so, surrenders its life and gutters out. Paul's picture of crucifixion with Christ, with its result that Christ's life is his own, is even more dramatic. It expressed a reality which was at the very heart of his preaching, his ministry, his total experience. "I have been crucified with Christ: the life I now live is not my life, but the life which Christ lives in me; and my present bodily life is lived by faith in the Son of God."[6]

Brendel's passion not "to be in the way"; Schnabel's passion to "think of Beethoven and then he will play"; Newman's passion to "disappear into the reality of which he spoke" are but illustrations of Paul's basic principle – his passionate hope that "I shall have no cause to be ashamed, but shall speak so boldly that now as always the greatness of Christ will shine out clearly in my person, whether through my life or through my death."[7] It was thus that he allowed us to hear the voice and to discern the mind of the Master.

To draw out the relevance of what we have just

written to the task of the Christian preacher would be to insult the reader's intelligence. But the musicians have so much to teach the preachers that one further point may be allowed. In an interview on television between Levin and Brendel,[8] Levin asked the pianist about the inter-action of pianist and audience during a recital. Brendel replied that it was "like an electric stream that goes into the audience and comes back again, and *greatly enhances what the pianist does.*" In fact, the effectiveness of the pianist's rendering depends not only on *him* but on *them.* This is abundantly true of preaching – for preaching, if it is true preaching, should be an act of co-operative worship, what P. T. Forsyth called "the organised Hallelujah of an ordered community".[9] It is a combined operation.

I have written about this elsewhere.[10] Suffice it here to say that preaching is not simply the function of the man or woman up there in the pulpit. It is the function of the *Church* gathered in that place for worship. The preacher offers to God the distillation of his prayer, thought, agonising, writing, during the preceding days of preparation. The members of the congregation offer to God their minds, their openness to truth, their alert-ness to receive, their willingness to respond. They go to work together, seeking to make an offering not too unworthy of the God whose grace they receive both in the sacrament of the Eucharist and in the sacrament of the Word. For, in the preaching, the man in the pulpit and the people in the pew are engaged in "sharing a series of discoveries". In preaching, the preacher does not throw out a series of pre-digested truths for his listeners to swallow, like a mother-bird feeding her young with re-gurgitated nourishment. On the con-trary, he bids his congregation engage with him in "exploration into God". That is their joint enterprise. As they engage in it together, there is *mutual* benefit and strengthening. "I long to see you", Paul wrote to the Romans; "I want to bring you some spiritual gift to make you strong; or, rather, I want to be among you *to be myself encouraged by your faith as well as you by mine.*"[11]

> The human heart can go to the lengths of God.
> Dark and cold we may be, but this
> Is no winter now. The frozen misery
> Of centuries breaks, cracks, begins to move;
> The thunder is the thunder of the floes,
> The thaw, the flood, the upstart Spring.
> Thank God our time is now when wrong
> Comes up to face us everywhere,
> Never to leave us till we take
> The longest stride of soul men ever took.
> Affairs are now soul size,
> The enterprise
> Is exploration into God.
> Where are you making for? It takes
> So many thousand years to wake,
> But will you wake for pity's sake.[12]

In seeking to understand Paul as, above all things, an interpreter of the mind of Christ, we have begun to understand the paradox of his letters. They have about them all the marks of the passing, the transient, the contemporary. They were sent to meet particular needs, to deal with particular problems, to correct particular misunderstandings. And yet – they have about them touches of the timeless, marks of eternity, which make them, in the main thrust of their message, as relevant to the needs of twentieth-century men and women as to those of their first-century readers. Explain this as we will, call it the inspiration of the Spirit as no doubt we should, the phenomenon is there, and we may thank God for it.

Written for small communities living in lands north of the Mediterranean Sea, the letters have a powerful word to say to the sophisticated and tired nations of modern Europe, to the materially prosperous and spiritually impoverished nations of North America and

West Africa, to the politically disturbed peoples of Latin America, and to the emerging nations of Asia.

If we ask how this can be, we may reply that for Paul, as for the writer of the book of the Revelation, a door had been opened in heaven and he had responded to the voice which said, "Come up here, and I will show you . . ."[13] From that vantage point, he could see things *sub specie aeternitatis*, and write with confidence of God and man, of truth and justice, of sin and judgement, of the temporal and of what is beyond time. As a faithful interpreter of the mind of Christ, a "fifth evangelist" concerned to manifest the Word incarnate, crucified, risen and glorified, he saw in the Body of Christ "God's pilot scheme for the final phase" . . . his "masterpiece of reconciliation", destined "to provide the pattern for the reconciled universe of the future, when all things will find their unity under Christ as their true head".[14]

To read the Pauline correspondence with any depth of perception is to lay oneself open to an invitation from the writer to join him in "exploration into God". It is an awe-full task, in the literal sense of the adjective. It has no fixed bounds, no nicely tied-up ends. And it is a task which can only be accomplished if at the same time the treasure at its heart is being shared. "It would be misery to me not to preach."[15] "To me, who am less than the least of all God's people, he has granted of his grace the privilege of proclaiming . . . the good news of the unfathomable riches of Christ."[16] To share in the exploration is to share in the mission. To share in the mission is to advance in the exploration.

It was this combination of exploration with mission that made Paul the man that he was.

Almighty God,
who caused the light of the gospel
    to shine throughout the world
through the preaching of your servant Saint Paul:
grant that we who celebrate his wonderful conversion
may follow him in bearing witness to your truth;
through Jesus Christ our Lord.

(Collect of The Conversion of Saint Paul,
Alternative Service Book, 1980)

NOTES TO TEXT

CHAPTER 1   YOUTH

1. Hodder and Stoughton, 1937
2. *Naturalis Historia*, xxvii 3
3. *On the Morning of Christ's Nativity*, 4
4. *op. cit.*, p.138
5. A. D. Nock: *St Paul* (O.U.P., 1938), p.97
6. *op. cit.*, p.94
7. Buchan, *op. cit.*, pp.286 and 287
8. Romans 15: 23–4
9. *Julius Caesar* IV, iii 217
10. Galatians 4: 4 (RSV)
11. Ephesians 2: 12
12. 1 Corinthians 8: 5
13. Acts 21: 39
14. Acts 18: 3
15. *Paul the Apostle* (Collins, 1981), pp.14 and 15
16. *Paul of Tarsus* (S.C.M., 1925), p.11
17. Philippians 3: 5–6
18. Acts 22: 3
19. Acts 5: 34
20. Galatians 1: 14
21. Acts 23: 16
22. Acts 22: 28
23. Acts 16: 37
24. Indira Gandhi: *India. The Speeches and Reminiscences of Indira Gandhi* (Hodder and Stoughton, 1975), p.63
25. Exodus 32
26. Nehemiah 1: 4 and 6
27. Daniel 9: 5 ff.
28. H. Wheeler Robinson: *Two Hebrew Prophets* (Lutterworth, 1948), pp.25 and 29
29. Luke 13: 34
30. Luke 19: 41–2
31. Isaiah 42: 6

32. Romans 9: 1–5 and 10: 1–3
33. Philippians 3: 10
34. See, for example, Acts 13: 44–52, and 18: 5–11
35. Acts 28: 16–28
36. Romans 11: 32
37. Romans 11: 33 and 36
38. 1 Corinthians 15: 25 and 28

CHAPTER 2 NEW CREATION
 1. Chapters 9, 22 and 26
 2. Luke 13: 34
 3. Luke 2: 41–52
 4. Acts 7: 54–60 and 8: 1
 5. Acts 6: 5, 8 and 15
 6. Acts 7: 54 ff.
 7. L. Grollenberg: *Paul* (S.C.M., 1978), pp.36–7
 8. Acts 9: 1–2
 9. Acts 26: 9–11 (Phillips)
10. Galatians 1: 13
11. 2 Corinthians 4: 5–6
12. Genesis 1: 1–4
13. 2 Corinthians 5: 17
14. Philippians 3: 12
15. Phillips
16. Philippians 3: 13 (AV)
17. *Confessions* II, 1, i. "My very being was torn asunder because I turned away from Thee, the One, and wasted myself upon the many" (F. J. Sheed's translation)
18. 2 Corinthians 5: 14
19. *Journal* (1889–1915), translation by Justin O'Brien
20. Romans 8: 29
21. *Confessions* VIII, 12
22. *A Third Testament* (Collins and BBC, 1977), p.29
23. *The Seven Storey Mountain* (Sheldon, 1975), p.123
24. *op. cit.*, pp.204–7
25. The phrase is taken from John Masefield's "The Everlasting Mercy", in which he tells the story of the conversion of Saul Kane.
26. BBC Broadcast, 27 March, 1982
27. From his *Introduction* to *What I Believe* (O.U.P. World's Classics, 1940), p.307

28. Acts 26: 16–18
29. Grollenberg, *op. cit.*, pp.37–8

CHAPTER 3   FRUITFUL DESERT
1. Acts 22: 10
2. Acts 9: 10–16
3. Acts 9: 26–7
4. *Finally: With Paul to the End* (Hodder and Stoughton, 1935), p.129
5. Acts 9: 18–22
6. Galatians 1: 16–17
7. On this, see further chapter 9, pp.170ff.
8. Isaiah 42: 1–4; 49: 1–6; 50: 4–11; 52: 13– 53: 12
9. 1 Kings 19: 4–13
10. Amos 1: 1 and 7: 14–15
11. Mark 1: 4–5
12. Mark 1: 12–13
13. Constable, 1936
14. Seabury Press, pp. 43–4
15. *The Sign of Jonas* (Doubleday, 1956), p.311
16. *The Seven Storey Mountain*, p.304
17. *A Camel in the Needle's Eye* (S.C.M., 1981), p.178
18. Psalm 40: 1
19. Psalm 130: 5–6
20. Isaiah 40: 30–1
21. Galatians 1: 17–18
22. 2 Corinthians 11: 32
23. *A Man in Christ* (Hodder and Stoughton, 1935), p.132
24. F. W. H. Myers: *St Paul*

CHAPTER 4   A CHARACTER
1. Any date more precise than this is bound to be in the nature of conjecture, as a glance at the guesses of scholars makes clear.
2. *The Journeys of St Paul* (Hamlyn, 1973), p.13
3. See Romans 15: 23
4. See his *The Church in the Roman Empire* (Hodder and Stoughton, 1897), p.375 ff.
5. 2 Corinthians 10: 10
6. See, for example, Acts 9: 29; 16: 25–8; 19: 30

7. Acts 16: 28
8. Acts 16: 1 ff.; 18: 18 ff.; 19: 21
9. Acts 27
10. Acts 16: 16–18
11. Acts 16: 35–9. There is something of a parallel in the case of Pope Shenouda III, of the Coptic Church, who was confined to his monastery by the late President Sadat. He refused to leave the monastery and to resume his former extensive ministry unless and until the Government would openly declare that he had been wrongly detained.
12. Acts 23: 1–5
13. Acts 15: 36–41. Young Mark was probably sensitive and homesick, and Paul may well have had a bout of malaria!
14. Romans 3: 27
15. 2 Corinthians 11: 16–17
16. vv. 7–11
17. 1 Corinthians 15: 31; 2 Corinthians 7: 4 and 14; and 8: 24
18. Romans 5: 3
19. Galatians 1: 8–9
20. Galatians 2: 12
21. I owe this suggestion to T. W. Manson: *The Teaching of Jesus* (C.U.P., 1931), pp.241–2.
22. Galatians 3: 1 (Phillips); 5: 12
23. Galatians 4: 14
24. Acts 20: 36–8
25. Acts 21: 1–14
26. Galatians 4: 19–20 (Phillips)
27. Galatians 4: 19
28. Romans 8: 29
29. 1 Corinthians 4: 14–15 and 21. Donald Nicholl defines a "soul-friend" as "one who combines the firmness and austerity expected of a father with the gentleness and warmth expected of a mother". *Holiness* (Darton, Longman and Todd, 1981), p.118
30. 1 Thessalonians 2: 1–12
31. Philemon 10–11
32. Philippians 1: 8
33. See Acts 16: 11 ff.
34. Philippians 1: 25

35. Philippians 4: 1
36. Romans 16: 1–2, 13, 16
37. Günther Bornkamm: *Paul* (Hodder and Stoughton, 1971), p.84
38. Ephesians 3: 8
39. The form of the word is strange – a comparative piled on top of a superlative! The only occurrence of it in Liddell and Scott's *Greek–English Lexicon* (eighth edition, 1929) is from the passage here under discussion.
40. Acts 8: 1
41. *St Francis of Assisi* (Frederick Muller, 1981), p.58
42. *Catherine of Siena* (Sheed and Ward, 1954), p.135
43. Isaiah 6, and see 2 Chronicles 26
44. Exodus 3: 10–12; 4: 1 ff.
45. Jeremiah 1: 4–10
46. Amos 7: 14
47. 2 Corinthians 4: 7
48. 2 Corinthians 12: 10
49. 2 Corinthians 11: 23–7. How can J. A. Hutton call Paul "delicate"? (*Finally: With Paul to the End*, pp.53 and 54)
50. *The Divine Comedy, Inferno*, Canto 6, ll.107–8
51. *Conversations with Menuhin* (St Martin's Press, New York, 1980), p.15
52. See chapter 5, pp.89ff.
53. *St Paul: A Study in Social and Religious History* (Hodder and Stoughton, 1912), p.128
54. Romans 8: 29
55. Romans 8: 5–6
56. Philippians 1: 21 (Phillips)
57. Galatians 2: 20
58. Acts 9: 18
59. 1 Corinthians 1: 14
60. On the corporate aspect of the phrase "in Christ", see further chapter 9, pp.173ff.
61. 2 Corinthians 5: 17 (NEB note j)
62. Colossians 1: 13
63. *Christianity according to St Paul* (C.U.P., 1927), pp.16–18
64. Romans 5: 1 (AV)
65. John 15
66. See, for example, Psalm 80: 8 ff.; Isaiah 5: 1–7; Jeremiah 2: 20 ff.

67. 1 Corinthians 12: 12. And note C. F. D. Moule: 1 Cor: 12
    12 ff. and 6: 15 "are difficult to interpret otherwise than
    as symptoms of a mode of thought which viewed Christ
    himself as an inclusive Person, a Body, to be joined to
    which was to become part of him." *The Origin of Christ-
    ology* (C.U.P., 1977), p.81
68. Kegan Paul, Trench, Trubner, 1927
69. Romans 3: 23
70. Psalm 8: 5 (AV) ("little less than a god", NEB)
71. *Heauton Timorumenos*, 1, i, 25
72. *Book of Common Prayer*, Collect of Good Friday
73. William Temple: *Citizen and Churchman* (Eyre and
    Spottiswood, 1941), pp.74–5
74. Romans 11: 33, 36
75. Ephesians 3: 20–1
76. Galatians 1: 4–5
77. *The Creator Spirit* (Martin Hopkinson, London, 1928),
    p.218
78. Clearly he has in mind such passages as Colossians 3:
    9–10 and Galatians 2: 20.

CHAPTER 5   GROWTH
1. 1 Thessalonians 2: 14–16
2. Romans 9: 2–5; 10: 1; 11: 1–2
3. 1 Thessalonians 4: 15. Cp. 1 Corinthians 7: 29–31; and
   15: 51 – "we shall not all die" (NEB); "sleep" (AV)
4. The doctrines of the Church and of the consummation of
   all things in Christ take a larger place in his later
   writings and the second advent a smaller one.
5. Philippians 3: 8 (AV)
6. Acts 18: 3
7. 2 Corinthians 11: 26–7. Adolf Deissmann has a vivid
   description of Paul's journeyings as seen through Deissmann's eyes during his travels over the same ground in
   the early years of this century. See his *St Paul: A Study
   in Social and Religious History*, pp.64–6, and cp. the
   equally vivid descriptions of that intrepid traveller and
   disciple and colleague of Sir William Ramsay, Gertrude
   Bell, in *The Letters of Gertrude Bell*, Vol. I, selected and
   edited by Lady Bell, D.B.E., (Penguin Books, 1927). Her
   travels took place in 1905 and 1907, and her descrip-

tions of "the great snows of Taurus", of the Cilician plain, and the journey to Konia ("too boiling and too hot") are well worth reading (see especially chapter 10).

8. 2 Timothy 2: 3 (AV)
9. 2 Corinthians 12: 1–10
10. *Werke: Kritische Gesamtausgabe* 54, 16
11. Galatians 4: 14 (NEB note u)
12. *Finally: With Saint Paul to the End*, p.26
13. Daniel 3: 25 (Jerusalem Bible)
14. Isaiah 43: 2 (AV)
15. Ian Hunter: *Malcolm Muggeridge: A Life* (Collins, 1980), p.58
16. 2 Corinthians 7: 10
17. *The Joy of the Snow* (Hodder and Stoughton, 1976), p.196
18. Frank Lake in *Contact* 1980: 3 (*The Theology of Pastoral Counselling*)
19. Diana Dewar: *Saint of Auschwitz* (Darton, Longman and Todd, 1982), p.46
20. *ibid.*, p.105
21. Quoted from Milton's *Defensio Secunda* by A. N. Wilson in his *Life of John Milton* (O.U.P., 1983), p.175
22. 2 Corinthians 11: 23–7
23. Acts 15: 38
24. 2 Timothy 4: 10
25. 2 Corinthians 2: 4
26. Galatians 3: 1 (Phillips)
27. Robin Daniels: *Conversations with Cardus* (Gollancz, 1976), p.270
28. 2 Corinthians 4: 16–18
29. Romans 8: 18 ff. And see further chapter 10
30. Acts 9, 22 and 26. See above chapter 2, pp.45–6
31. See above chapter 3, p.56
32. Isaiah 42: 6–7
33. Isaiah 49: 6; cp. also 19: 24–5 – "Israel shall rank with Egypt and Assyria, those three, and shall be a blessing in the centre of the world. . . ."
34. Isaiah 66: 20–1
35. See, for example, Psalm 65: 5, Zechariah 8: 20–3 and 14: 8–19, and Zephaniah 3: 9–10
36. *St Paul*, p.85
37. Acts 16: 6–10

38. Acts 19: 21
39. H. V. Morton: *In the Steps of St Paul* (Rich and Cowan, 1936), p.58
40. Chapters 10 and 12

CHAPTER 6   THINKER AND WRITER
 1. Job 11: 7–8 (AV)
 2. 1 Corinthians 8: 1–2
 3. 1 Corinthians 13: 2 and 8
 4. Galatians 1: 12
 5. 1 Corinthians 1: 21
 6. 1 Corinthians 3: 19
 7. 2 Corinthians 4: 6; cp. Galatians 4: 9 where Paul is hesitant to speak of "knowing God" and prefers the concept of being "known by God".
 8. Philippians 3: 8–10
 9. Colossians 1: 9–10
10. Ephesians 4: 13
11. *Of the Imitation of Christ*, II, 1
12. Robin Daniels: *Conversations with Cardus*, p.14
13. Romans 2: 4
14. 2 Corinthians 7: 10
15. 2 Corinthians 12: 21
16. Romans 12: 2
17. Matthew 17: 2; Mark 9: 2
18. 2 Corinthians 3: 12–18
19. Philippians 4: 8
20. Philippians 2: 5 ff.
21. 1 Corinthians 2: 16 (AV)
22. C. A. Anderson Scott: *New Testament Ethics* (C.U.P., 1934), p.83
23. *ibid.*, p.102
24. 2 Corinthians 10: 5 (RSV)
25. 1 Peter 1: 13 (AV)
26. Dom Adrian Morey: *David Knowles: A Memoir* (Darton, Longman and Todd, 1979), p.136
27. Gordon S. Wakefield, in his introduction to *Crucifixion – Resurrection: The Pattern of the Theology and Ethics of the New Testament* (S.P.C.K., 1981), p.51
28. James Brabazon: *Dorothy L. Sayers: A Biography* (Gollancz, 1981), p.166

29. *ibid.*, p.169
30. *ibid.*, p.213
31. *ibid.*, pp.254–5
32. *ibid.*, pp.262–3. After writing this chapter, I came across a strangely similar passage in A. N. Wilson's *Life of John Milton*. Wilson said of his subject: "Nothing in his poems, although he was technically a Christian of sorts, suggests the very slightest warmth of feeling about the person of Christ. Unlike Herbert, Milton never brings to God 'the cream of all his heart' still less does he call God 'my dear'. He brings to God a fearless and impersonal pursuit of the truth and a mind over-brimmed with reading." (p.136)
33. *ibid.*, p.265
34. Galatians 2: 20
35. Philippians 3: 20
36. James Brabazon: *op. cit.*, p.225
37. 1 Corinthians 9: 16
38. 2 Corinthians 5: 20
39. Philippians 3: 13 (AV)
40. Peter Brent: *Charles Darwin: "A man of enlarged curiosity"* (Heinemann, 1981), p.342
41. *ibid.*, p.462
42. *ibid.*, p.477
43. *ibid.*, p.188
44. *ibid.*, p.369
45. *ibid.*, p.315
46. *ibid.*, p.514
47. *ibid.*, p.342
48. 1 Corinthians 1: 24 and 30 (AV)
49. 1 Corinthians 1, especially 18 ff.
50. Günther Bornkamm: *Paul*, pp.159–60
51. 2 Corinthians 10: 5
52. Romans 15: 5
53. Colossians 2: 8
54. Colossians 2: 2
55. 2 Corinthians 3: 14
56. As in Mark 6: 52 and 8: 17
57. 2 Corinthians 6: 1
58. T. R. Glover: *Paul of Tarsus*, p.97
59. *ibid.*, p.110
60. John 2: 24–5

61. *Canterbury Cathedral Chronicle*, 1980, p.23
62. See further chapter 7, pp.128–9; and my *The Prayers of the New Testament* (Mowbray, 1984), especially p.98.
63. Antonio de Pérez-Esclarin: *Atheism and Liberation* (S.C.M., 1980), p.199
64. Brian Martin: *John Henry Newman, his life and work* (Chatto and Windus, 1982), p.143
65. *ibid.*, p.142
66. See further chapter 4, p.68
67. 1 Corinthians 7: 25; 8: 1; 8: 4; 12: 1; 16: 1
68. Galatians 4: 21 ff.
69. 1 Corinthians 10: 1 ff.
70. Deuteronomy 25: 4
71. 1 Corinthians 9: 9 ff.
72. Romans 16: 22
73. Shakespeare: *Julius Caesar* I, ii
74. Günther Bornkamm: *op. cit.*, p.xxvi

CHAPTER 7 MAN OF PRAYER

1. Romans 9: 4
2. Romans 8: 14–17
3. Romans 5: 2 (AV)
4. Ephesians 2: 18; 3: 12
5. Quoted in J. C. Beker; *Paul the Apostle: The Triumph of God in Life and Thought* (Fortress Press, 1980), p.355
6. T. A. Smail: *The Forgotten Father* (Hodder and Stoughton, 1980), p.42, italics mine
7. Ephesians 3: 12
8. For example, in 2 Corinthians 7: 4 and Ephesians 6: 19
9. Hebrews 4: 16; 10: 19
10. 1 John 3: 21; cp. 5: 14
11. 2 Corinthians 12: 1–10
12. Oliver Tomkins: *The Life of Edward Woods* (S.C.M., 1957), p.35; and see further chapter 5, pp.89ff.
13. Romans 8: 26 ff.
14. Friedrich Heiler: *Prayer: A study in the History and Psychology of Religion* (O.U.P., 1932), p.iv
15. Luke 10: 40
16. *God as Spirit* (Clarendon Press, 1977), p.87–8; and cp. Frank Lake: "The Holy Spirit ... attends ... to the

communications" (*Tight Corners in Pastoral Counselling* (Darton, Longman and Todd, 1981), p.46

17. Romans 8: 34
18. *God as Spirit* (Clarendon Press, Oxford, 1977), p.5
19. M. Ramsey: *Be Still and Know* (Collins, 1982), pp.53–4, cp. also p.73. See, further, C. F. D. Moule's important chapter "The Sacrifice of the People of God" in his *Essays in New Testament Interpretation* (C.U.P., 1982), pp.287 ff.
20. B. F. Westcott: *The Epistle to the Hebrews* (Macmillan, 1892), p.192
21. *Spirit of Flame* (S.C.M., 1943), p.101
22. *The Prayers of the New Testament*, p.87
23. 1 Corinthians 16: 22
24. R. T. France: "The Uniqueness of Christ" in *Churchman*, Vol. 95, No.3, p.209. He is quoting from C. F. D. Moule: *The Origin of Christology*, p.41
25. See, for example, Romans 1: 9; Ephesians 1: 16; 1 Thessalonians 1: 2; Philemon 4
26. H. A. Williams: *Some Day I'll Find You* (Mitchell Beazley, 1982), pp.364 and 366
27. Romans 1: 9; 1 Thessalonians 1: 2; 2: 13; 5: 17
28. See, for example, Philippians 4: 6 and Colossians 4: 2
29. See above, p.126
30. *Letters to Malcolm Chiefly on Prayer* (Geoffrey Bles, 1963) pp.92–3
31. From T. Binney's hymn: "Eternal Light, eternal Light, how pure the soul must be . . ."

CHAPTER 8   FREEDOM-FIGHTER

1. 2 Corinthians 3: 17
2. The tractate *Aboth* (*The Fathers*), in the Mishnah, says that the prophets committed the Law "to the men of the Great Synagogue, who said three things: Be deliberate in judgement, raise up many disciples, and *make a fence around the Law*" (1, i)
3. Romans 8: 2
4. *The Fifth Evangelist* (S.C.M., 1980), p.24
5. Romans 7: 24–5
6. Galatians 5: 1 NEB note z
7. Galatians 2: 20

8. *Some Day I'll Find You*, p.360
9. John 8: 36
10. Romans 8: 2
11. Galatians 5: 14
12. Romans 5: 5
13. See above chapter 6, pp.112ff.
14. 2 Corinthians 5: 9
15. 1 Corinthians 11: 1 (AV)
16. Galatians 5: 19–23 (AV)
17. Matthew 7: 16
18. Mark 4: 3 ff.
19. Luke 13: 6 ff.
20. *The Seven Storey Mountain*, pp.237–8
21. Psalm 42: 2
22. *Out of Solitude* (Ave Maria Press, 1974), p.42
23. C. A. A. Scott's division of the nine into three triplets is note-worthy – (1) those at the centre, Love, Joy, Serenity, (2) those nearer the surface, Long-temperedness, Good Feeling, Generosity, (3) those on the surface, Good Faith, Courtesy, Self-Control (*St Paul, the Man and the Teacher* (C.U.P., 1936), p.132
24. See chapter 11, pp.214ff.
25. *Works* III, 296
26. Psalm 103: 13
27. Hosea 11: 1–4
28. On this see further W. H. Vanstone: *The Stature of Waiting* (Darton, Longman and Todd, 1982), especially pp.91 ff., where he allows the idea of God's passibility in the sense that "the glory of God . . . appears at its deepest level when the activity of God achieves the exposure of God. . . ." (p.94). And see further "*A Hymn to the Creator*" in his *Love's Endeavour Love's Expense* (Darton, Longman and Todd, 1977), pp.119–20. The last verse runs:

> Thou art God; no monarch thou
> Thron'd in easy state to reign,
> Thou art God, Whose arms of love
> Aching, spent, the world sustain.

cp. also Simone Weil: "The love of God for us is a passion. How could that which is good love that which is evil without suffering? And that which is evil suffers too in loving that which is good. The mutual love of God and man is suffering." (*Gravity and Grace*, p.81)

29. *Pray to Live* (Fides Publishers, Inc., 1972), p.66
30. Matthew 19: 19 and Galatians 5: 14
31. Luke 10: 21
32. John 15: 11
33. John 17: 13
34. Matthew 5: 3 ff.
35. See, for example, Psalm 1: 1–3; 19: 7–11; 119 *passim*
36. Deuteronomy 14: 22 ff.
37. *The Divine Comedy – Paradiso*, Canto 33
38. Sigrid Undset: *Catherine of Siena*, p.135
39. Romans 5: 2
40. 1 Corinthians 13: 13
41. 1 Thessalonians 1: 3
42. *Out of Solitude*, p.59
43. Philippians 1: 23 ff.
44. Romans 5: 3–5
45. Galatians 6: 17
46. 2 Corinthians 12: 1–10
47. Isaiah 57: 20–1
48. For examples, see pp.154–5
49. Luke 7: 50
50. Luke 8: 35
51. Luke 19: 2–9
52. Romans 14: 17
53. Ephesians 2: 14–16
54. Romans 5: 1–2. I prefer "we have peace" rather than "let us have peace", as being truer to the context. Anders Nygren argues forcefully for this in his *Commentary on Romans* (S.C.M., 1952), pp.193–4
55. Philippians 4: 7
56. *The Joy of the Snow*, p.206
57. 1 Corinthians 13: 4
58. *Hymn of the Universe* (Collins, 1965), pp.76–7
59. Romans 11: 36
60. Robert Speaight: *Teilhard de Chardin: A Biography* (Collins, 1967), p.227
61. Romans 2: 4
62. Romans 9: 23
63. 1 Timothy 1: 16–17

64. I have developed this a little more fully in my *Mission to the World* (Hodder and Stoughton, 1981), pp.32 ff.
65. Ephesians 2: 7; 5: 9
66. 2 Corinthians 6: 6
67. Romans 3: 27
68. Galatians 1: 23
69. *Paul*, p.141
70. See further chapter 11, pp.208ff.
71. The word is used in this particular sense, if the New English Bible rendering is correct, in 1 Timothy 2: 15 (note c) – "if only husband and wife continue in *mutual fidelity*".
72. Romans 15: 5
73. 2 Thessalonians 3: 5; there is no reference to the Second Advent here, as the Authorised Version rendering suggests.
74. 2 Timothy 2: 12
75. Hebrews 12: 2
76. John Buchan: *Mr Standfast*
77. Elizabeth Goudge: *The Joy of the Snow*, p.229
78. 2 Corinthians 10: 1
79. Philippians 2: 8
80. 1 Corinthians 7: 9
81. 1 Corinthians 9: 25
82. Acts 24: 25
83. Romans 8: 18–22
84. Amos 4: 1–3
85. Isaiah 3: 14–15
86. Luke 10: 29 ff. and Matthew 25: 31 ff.
87. James 5: 1
88. Romans 1: 18
89. John Buchan: *Augustus*, p.207
90. Exodus 21: 5
91. Colossians 3: 22–5
92. Ephesians 6: 5–9
93. Luke 3: 14
94. Ecclesiastes 3: 7
95. Philemon 16
96. *Dunamis* by G. Betty Hares, quoted by Elizabeth Bassett in *Each in his Prison* (S.P.C.K., 1978), p.313
97. Galatians 3: 28 (Phillips)
98. Quoted by Malcolm Muggeridge and Alec Vidler in

Paul, Envoy Extraordinary (Collins, 1972), p.11

99. C. A. A. Scott: *St Paul, The Man and The Teacher*, pp.132 and 133
100. *Babylonian Talmud: Yebamoth*, 63b
101. 1 Corinthians 7: 15
102. Philippians 3: 8
103. 1 Corinthians 7, 29 and 32–35
104. W. M. Ramsay: *The Cities of St Paul* (Hodder and Stoughton, 1907), pp.204–5. Those who wish to pursue further the position of women in the first-century world and in particular at Corinth should consult an article by Gillian Clark, "The Women at Corinth", in *Theology* (July 1982, pp.256ff.).
105. 1 Corinthians 14: 34–5
106. 1 Corinthians 11: 5
107. See note 104 above
108. *Theological Investigations Volume 20: Concern for the Church* (Darton, Longman and Todd, 1981), pp.36 and 42. And see further George Carey: *Women and Authority in the Church: A Scriptural Perspective* (Movement for the Ordination of Women, 1983)
109. Galatians 3: 28
110. E. F. Scott: *The Nature of the Early Church* (Charles Scribner's Sons, 1941), p.168
111. See especially Ephesians 5: 22–4 and cp. 1 Corinthians 11: 3
112. Lindsay Dewar: *An Outline of Christian Ethics* (University of London Press: Hodder and Stoughton, 1949), pp.140–1
113. L. S. Thornton: *The Common Life in the Body of Christ* (Dacre Press, 1942), p.222

CHAPTER 9   CHURCHMAN

1. Philippians 3: 5
2. Deuteronomy 23: 2
3. A. D. Nock; *St Paul*, p.48
4. Mark 13: 1
5. Romans 9: 4
6. C. F. D. Moule: "A Christian Understanding of Law and Grace", in *Christian Jewish Relations*, vol. 14 Number 1, March 1981, pp.54–5; italics mine

7. Hosea 2: 14–17
8. Jeremiah 3: 6–7
9. Ezekiel 16
10. Isaiah 62: 5
11. Romans 10: 9
12. Romans 12: 4–5
13. Ephesians 4: 4
14. Colossians 1: 24
15. Claude Chavasse: *The Bride of Christ: An Enquiry into the Nuptial Element in Early Christianity* (Faber and Faber, 1940) has much useful material on this theme.
16. See especially 1 Corinthians 12: 12 ff., Romans 12: 3 ff. and Ephesians 4: 1–16
17. Ephesians 2: 20–2
18. F. W. Dillistone: *The Structure of the Divine Society* (Lutterworth Press, 1951), p.69
19. On the corporate aspect of being "in Christ", see chapter 4, pp.77ff.
20. 1 Corinthians 2: 16
21. *The Parting of Friends* (John Murray, 1966), p.2
22. *ibid.*, p.21
23. John Pollock: *Wilberforce* (Constable, 1977), p.220
24. J. S. Pobee: *Towards an African Theology* (Abingdon/Nashville, 1979), p.49
25. For a further development of this theme, see Lesslie Newbigin: *The Open Secret* (S.P.C.K., 1978)
26. 1 Corinthians 6: 11 (RV)
27. Ephesians 5: 26
28. 1 Corinthians 11: 23 ff.
29. vv.29 and 30
30. 1 Corinthians 1: 10 ff.
31. 1 Corinthians 3: 1 ff.
32. 1 Corinthians 5: 1 ff.
33. 1 Corinthians 6: 1 ff.
34. 2 Corinthians 11: 28 (AV)
35. 1 Corinthians 1: 23
36. John D. Davies: *Beginning Now: Contemporary Experience of Creation and Fall* (Collins, 1971), p.170
37. Acts 9: 17–19, 23–25
38. Acts 14: 19–20
39. Acts 13: 1–3
40. Acts 14: 26–15: 3

41. Romans 15: 24, 28–29

CHAPTER 10   MAN OF VISION
1. Chapter 8, p.144
2. 1 Corinthians 13: 13
3. 1 Corinthians 15: 57
4. Philippians 1: 21–6
5. 2 Corinthians 4: 16–5: 10
6. 1 Corinthians 8: 5 (AV)
7. Ephesians 2: 12
8. 1 Corinthians 1: 28; 2: 6
9. Philippians 2: 15–16
10. F. W. Dillistone, writing of Max Warren in his biography, *Into all the World* (Hodder and Stoughton, 1980), p.80. See also my *Mission to the World*, pp.30 ff.
11. Romans 6: 23
12. Romans 8: 20 ff.
13. Romans 8: 19, 23
14. Romans 8: 28, 38–9
15. Colossians 1: 13–20
16. Romans 11: 36
17. 1 Corinthians 15: 28
18. Ephesians 1: 9–10
19. A. R. Peacocke: *Creation and the World of Science* (O.U.P., 1979), pp.244–5
20. *Paul the Apostle: The Triumph of God in Life and Thought*, p.19
21. *ibid.*, p.363
22. *ibid.*, p.364
23. *ibid.*, p.366
24. T. F. Torrance: *Christian Theology and Scientific Culture* (Christian Journals Limited, 1980), pp.76–7
25. Revelation 21 and 22
26. *Teilhard de Chardin: A Biography*, pp.37–8
27. *ibid.*, p.102
28. Ephesians 1: 10. I owe the paraphrase to Donald Nicholl: *Holiness*, p.19.

CHAPTER 11   PAUL AND JESUS
1. See above chapter 10, pp.186ff.

2. Günther Bornkamm: *Paul*, p.110
3. *ibid.*, p.118
4. Romans 9: 4
5. Mark 7: 19
6. See, for example, Leviticus 11 and Deuteronomy 14
7. Mark 7: 17–23
8. Galatians 1: 14
9. Galatians 2: 12
10. Matthew 8: 5–13 = Luke 7: 1–10
11. Mark 7: 24–30
12. Luke 13: 29–30
13. F. C. N. Hicks: *The Fulness of Sacrifice* (S.P.C.K., 1959), pp.189–90
14. *The Cross and the Prodigal: The 15th chapter of Luke, seen through the eyes of Middle Eastern peasants* (Concordia Publishing House, St Louis, Missouri, 1973), p.9
15. *ibid.*, p.57
16. A. D. Nock: *St Paul*, p.128
17. I. H. Marshall: *The Gospel of Luke* (Paternoster Press, 1978), pp.694–5
18. Galatians 3: 26–8
19. Romans 16: 26
20. *A Man in Christ*, p.253
21. Romans 3: 26; 4: 5 with 8: 33; 8: 30.
22. *Paul*, p.237
23. Luke 5: 20
24. Luke 7: 9
25. Luke 7: 50; 8: 48; 17: 19; 18: 42
26. The phrase is C. A. A. Scott's in *St Paul, the Man and the Teacher*, pp.96–7
27. Romans 1: 17; 3: 26 (NEB); Ephesians 2: 8 (RSV)
28. Quoted by Professor J. G. Davies in *G. W. H. Lampe: A Memoir by Friends*, edited by C. F. D. Moule (Mowbray, 1982), p.49
29. pp.180 and 182
30. Galatians 2: 20 (AV)
31. Philippians 3: 9
32. *The Central Message of the New Testament* (Scribners, 1965), p.56
33. Quoted in A. M. Hunter: *The Fifth Evangelist*, p.10
34. Luke 7: 50; Romans 5: 1
35. Luke 19: 14 (AV)

36. T. W. Manson: *The Teaching of Jesus*, p.91; see also
    T. A. Smail: *The Forgotten Father*, especially pp.34–6
37. Especially in his *Abba* in *The Prayers of Jesus* (1967)
    and his *Abba as an Address to God* in his *New Testament Theology*, Vol. I (1971), pp.61 ff. and *The Central Message of the New Testament*, pp.9 ff.
38. Mark 15: 34 (AV)
39. *The Central Message of the New Testament*, p.21
40. *ibid.*, pp.27 and 28–9
41. Galatians 4: 6
42. Romans 8: 14 ff.
43. *The Forgotten Father*, p.41
44. *The Church, the Gospel and Society* (London, 1962), p.84
45. *op. cit.*, p.70
46. *Paul the Apostle*, p.131
47. *op. cit.*, pp.298 and 18
48. Acts 28: 7–9
49. Acts 27: 33 ff.
50. 1 Corinthians 12: 9
51. 2 Corinthians 5: 20
52. Matthew 22: 34–40
53. *Crucifixion-Resurrection: The Pattern of the Theology and Ethics of the New Testament*, p.117
54. Romans 5: 5
55. L. Grollenberg: *Paul*, p.125
56. Acts 7: 60 and 8: 1 (AV)
57. Acts 9: 17
58. Matthew 5: 38 ff.; 1 Corinthians 6: 7 ff.
59. Matthew 6: 25 ff.; Philippians 4: 6–7
60. Matthew 5: 44; Romans 12: 14
61. Galatians 5: 6
62. *Letters* (Edinburgh, 1877), p.16

CHAPTER 12   INVITATION TO EXPLORATION
1. 30 April, 1983
2. Owen Chadwick: *Newman* (O.U.P., 1983), p.21
3. 1 Corinthians 15: 31
4. Romans 6: 11 (Phillips)
5. John 3: 30 (AV)
6. Galatians 2: 20
7. Philippians 1: 20

8. July, 1982
9. P. T. Forsyth: *Positive Preaching and the Modern Mind* (Hodder and Stoughton, 1907), p.95
10. See my *Stewards of Grace* (Hodder and Stoughton, 1958), pp.85 ff.
11. Romans 1: 11–12
12. Christopher Fry: *A Sleep of Prisoners: A Play* (O.U.P., 1951)
13. Revelation 4: 1
14. F. F. Bruce: *Paul and Jesus* (Baker Book House, Grand Rapids, Michigan, 1974), pp. 38–9
15. 1 Corinthians 9: 16
16. Ephesians 3: 8

INDEX OF NAMES

INDEX OF SCRIPTURE REFERENCES

OLD TESTAMENT

NEW TESTAMENT

254